THE TRAIN
OF
CONSEQUENCES

ONE MAN'S JOURNEY
OUT OF MENTAL ILLNESS

RODERICK KNIGHT

authorHOUSE®

AuthorHouse™
1663 Liberty Drive, Suite 200
Bloomington, IN 47403
www.authorhouse.com
Phone: 1-800-839-8640

First published by AuthorHouse 6/3/2008

ISBN: 978-1-4343-7444-8 (sc)
ISBN: 978-1-4343-7443-1 (hc)

Library of Congress Control Number: 2008902486

Printed in the United States of America
Bloomington, Indiana

This book is printed on acid-free paper.

Chapter One

Each morning that fateful summer, I would pause as I pulled out of the apartment complex, waiting for the traffic to clear so I could make a left toward campus and summer school classes. In front of me was a sign with an arrow pointing right that somehow must have always been registering through the turmoil in my mind. But this morning, July 14, 1990, as I was poised to turn left, I stared at the big "H" on the sign, and the words "Trauma Center" under it, and decided it would be a good idea to turn right instead.

I wanted to escape the phone calls and the feeling of being followed and known wherever I went- in class, while driving to the store, talking on the phone. I felt like I was constantly being monitored, that I was being brainwashed, set up, that people wanted me to leave school. I was getting on people's nerves with the skinhead look and the alumni baseball cap I was wearing all the time and my black "Members Only" jacket. They were fed up with my arrogant, cocky attitude. "There he is, the tough guy. Don't mess around with him." I had no freedom. After three months of hell, it had reached a boiling point. I began thinking I wanted to kill myself.

I remember parking my car and then finding myself in a room with a few doctors, telling them over and over I was going to kill myself. They didn't know that the only way I would have followed through was if there had been an easy way to do it. The doctors kept telling me they wanted to help me. Finally, they called the cops to keep me from fighting to get out of there. They could see I lifted weights and was a pretty big guy. They believed I could become violent and told me I had to go to the Psychiatric Unit. That wasn't my choice. They took responsibility for me at that point. My admittance became involuntary. All of a sudden, I was not just a prisoner of my mind, but I had lost all my freedoms.

So the cops got there and grabbed me. Not wanting a broken arm, I didn't resist. They led me through a tunnel-like pathway, up an elevator and right into what was eventually my biggest nightmare-my first of a series of stays in mental hospitals. When all my dreams had been coming true, how could I have ended up in this place?

About a month before I found myself in the lockup ward of the psychiatric hospital, a guy I knew approached me as I was walking to class: "What's wrong with you? Your father and uncle graduated from here. What about you?" Had he really said that, or was my mind playing tricks? Soon after, I threatened him for throwing my dad and uncle up at me. They had both gone to school at North Carolina, and so I had always hoped to go there, too.

Growing up, I was a big fan of North Carolina sports because of my dad and uncle's love of the school. I'd go down to North Carolina often with both of them for football and basketball games. I especially loved North Carolina basketball and their legendary coach. In fifth grade, I even went to basketball camp there. Many times while visiting, we'd go to a popular restaurant, which unfortunately burned down before my arrival as a junior. My dad and uncle would play their ukulele and banjo there sometimes. Once they played at half time during a football game.

For me, it was like having two of the same father, my uncle and dad were so much alike. I especially remember watching them play tennis together. They grew up in New York City, but eventually both settled in the suburbs, where I was born and still live.

I was just a regular kid. Nothing extraordinary happened growing up, nothing that would indicate in any way the catastrophic turn my life would take. The doctors who were treating me labeled me paranoid schizophrenic. Of course it is natural to speculate about what might have triggered my mental illness. Were there signs when I was younger?

Sometimes I go back to when I broke my leg in May of '84, when I was fourteen and a freshman in high school. A friend and I were playing a wiffle ball game at his house. I was pitching to him, and, at one point when I struck him out, he threw the bat at me. I jumped to avoid getting hit, but the bat hit me on the inside of the knee and broke my leg. I spent the rest of the school year and part of the summer on crutches and then in physical therapy. I still don't know if he threw the bat deliberately or not, but that broken leg changed the direction of my life. Before the accident, I was a somewhat happy kid, friends with the mainstream kids and very popular. After the accident, everything began to change.

Because of my broken leg, I missed my final year at camp, the best year, since it was a sports camp and the last year was when you could traditionally excel. I'd already gone for seven good summers. My two older brothers never had wanted to go away to camp, and I had wanted to since I was six years old. So this was a great loss for me. My cast didn't come off until camp was half over, and arriving late like that wasn't much fun. I couldn't adjust to going in the middle of the session. Everyone had already been there for a while, and I felt like an outsider. Besides, my activities were still restricted, so there wasn't much for me to do at an all sports camp.

After a couple of days, I took the bus home. I was happy to leave. Mentally, I just wasn't right. Sometime in the Fall, the owners of the camp called me and offered to let me come back the next summer and finish then. I was welcome, they said. But I didn't want to do anything that next summer, except take Drivers Education. I regret that decision. I would have been one of the better athletes. But I was still unhappy from my experience the summer before, and so I thought I'd just take it easy over the next summer, try to relax.

I wasn't ever really happy in high school. Returning to school for my sophomore year, I hadn't been able to shake off the feeling of being an outcast that having a broken leg and hobbling around on crutches made me feel. I was angry that such a thing had happened to me. Friendships were based on the camaraderie of sports, and I couldn't participate. I had tried out for the baseball team as a freshman. Got cut. Didn't try sophomore year because of my leg. Junior year tried out, left before tryouts ended. Senior year I got cut again. Other than that I didn't play sports. So I hung around the library during free time, doing my assignments instead of socializing. I couldn't shake the anger. I was unhappy and didn't know how to turn things around. My mind got messed up over the whole broken leg thing and stayed messed up for the rest of high school. Junior and senior years I got involved with a gang. Twice I was suspended for fighting. My parents said one more time, and I was in real trouble.

The three main things that got me through high school were the wrestler "Rowdy" Roddy Piper, the New York Mets baseball team and the band Mötley Crüe.

Every Saturday morning, I looked forward to watching wrestling matches and Roddy Piper's talk show, Piper's Pit, on television. For three or four years in the mid eighties, Piper was my idol. He was the greatest. I loved the way he spoke and the way he handled his opponents. I also saw a lot of his matches live in Madison Square Garden.

Piper was always the villain. He didn't care what people thought about him. A lot of people didn't like him. But he was still able to draw a crowd. He won just about all of his matches. He wasn't one of those seven foot, four hundred pound guys, so I could relate for that reason, too. He was probably 6'2", two hundred thirty or forty pounds. Bigger than me, but I could relate. I wasn't huge, but I worked out weight lifting. I never took wrestling, but my friends and I would wrestle each other sometimes.

Piper always thought of himself as an outcast, which I now identified with. He never finished high school and was basically on the streets at a young age, graduating from the school of hard knocks instead. He started in the wrestling business at age fifteen. I related to how he talked to people and just everything about him. He was my idol and my model. The wrestling was supposed to be phony, but those guys really got hurt. It was physical, and I liked the violence. Piper had a hip replacement and half his hearing was knocked out by a chain, but he was still great.

Growing up, I had been a pretty scrawny kid. Even so, I would get into fights. Kids didn't know who they were messing with. I was so scrappy that I never lost a fight. Maybe that's why I liked Roddy Piper. He reminded me of myself. He was violent, and I was violent, too. High school street fights, bars, drinking, fighting. But, for the people I hung around with in high school and the first year of college, violence was the in thing. You had to be tough. We were sort of like a mini gang. I'm not proud of it really, but it was actually just a part of growing up. I was never violent towards anyone in my family.

In the eighties, New York Mets center fielder, Mookie Wilson, was someone else I looked up to. I was a huge Mets fan. I liked his style of play. He was a winner. He came to play, and he was good under pressure. He had probably the biggest at bat in Mets history, when he came up to the plate in the tenth inning of game six of the 1986 World Series against the Boston Red Sox, with two outs and the Series on the line. After a string of pitches were fouled off, a wild pitch had tied the game during Wilson's turn at bat. Then he got the hit that won the game. His lightning speed on the bases was instrumental in helping the Mets win the World Series in seven games.

The example those two men set for me played an important role in helping me get through the nightmare of my hospitalizations.

Looking back, I was a pretty normal kid in high school, even if I wasn't part of the mainstream. I experimented a little with drugs, smoked my first joint when I was a senior. At first I did it because friends were. Sometimes it was fun. Sometimes it wasn't. Sometimes I would overdo it, and I'd have a headache. I would drive high. I'd come home and try to go to sleep, but I couldn't sleep with all the thoughts that were racing through my head because of the drug.

Still, even with the normal fights that guys got into, I never really got into any trouble until after graduation. The summer after high school, some guys were messing with my friend at a local swimming pool. We challenged them. They said, "Come follow us," and took us back to their house, where we got into a fight in their driveway. A few days later, we saw them again and went after them again. The fight was wild. That's when the police were called, and we were arrested. But then our parents talked with their parents. The police dropped the charges and sealed the records, so we didn't have to go to jail. I don't like writing about it, though such behavior followed me for a few more years. Luckily I've been through enough to grow out of that kind of behavior. I was a kid that didn't take life seriously. I was carefree and not grown up yet. I didn't realize what I was getting myself into with my behavior most of the time.

I had begun to be a good student senior year in high school, but my grade point average couldn't be raised enough to go to the school of my dreams- North Carolina. So, my first two years of college were at a college in suburban New York. The first year, I lived in the dorm and came home on weekends. The second year I commuted. So, I had an idea of what living away from home was like, but not what it was like to be going to school down South. The idea of attending two different schools was more appealing than remaining and graduating from one. However, I ended up attending four schools. Something I would have never imagined.

The first two years of college were pretty uneventful, although the last semester before transferring to North Carolina, I took a ten week boxing class two nights a week at a local community college, from March to May. After a few weeks of training and exercise, we would match people up and spar. As the class continued, we would increase the rounds we sparred. I proved to myself that I was tough enough by completing the class. We did roadwork, pull ups, jumped rope, punched the speed bag and heavy bag, and shadow boxed. I had minor thoughts of possibly continuing to box, but I was already accepted at North Carolina and would rather go there. I had worked hard to make sure I would be able to transfer to North Carolina my junior year and succeeded with a 3.3 grade point average. A lot of alcohol, a lot of pot. It made me talkative. But, when I got to North Carolina, things got interesting.

CHAPTER TWO

As I looked forward to heading down to North Carolina, I felt I had my head on pretty straight. I was looking forward to enjoying myself, studying, drinking a little beer, hanging out. If it was going to take me an extra year to graduate, I didn't care. This was where I'd always wanted to go, and I was going to have fun. I loved New York, but I also wanted to get out in the world and experience something else. I planned to major in Radio, Television and Motion Pictures. Don Imus was the main reason I wanted to get into radio. I found his style of radio exciting.

A couple of weeks before school started, my new roommate at North Carolina showed up out of the blue, driving down my street while I was riding my brother's mini bike. He was a nice guy. I showed him around the house but never thought to ask him to stay over. He actually drove all the way from North Carolina. But I wasn't sophisticated enough to have it occur to me to offer him some hospitality.

The night before I went to North Carolina, I had my first sexual experience. I had never dated in high school and didn't go to the prom. I was always hanging out with the guys. In the fifth grade, I had a girl friend. But I never learned how to treat a girl or handle a relationship. As a favor before leaving, a friend of mine introduced me to a female friend of his, and we started messing around. One thing led to another that night. She wasn't even anyone I knew. I was very happy to get it over with. Finally! I was nineteen years old already!

My dad and uncle and my oldest brother flew down with me to get me settled at North Carolina. I'm sure they were just as excited as I was. At the airport, the metal detector went off as the authorities were checking my luggage. In their search, they found a metal key chain that looked like brass knuckles. When he saw the key chain, the cop said, "Well, I can see where you are going to end up." It turned out that he was sort of right; though I didn't end up in jail, I did end up in a nut house. After a little protesting on my part, that it was just a key chain, I had to hand it over.

My first dorm was coed and academic. A lot of people were from out of state. My roommate was there when I arrived, and it was nice to already know him. One of my suite mates was into hardcore music. He wasn't really a "skin head," but he liked bands like Sick of It All. I was more into the bigger thrash metal bands like Slayer, Exodus, MegaDeth and some of the smaller bands like Sodom and Supultura as well. Basically, the music was about violence and drinking.

I liked my other suite mate, too, so things were starting off very positively. I volunteered to be athletic director of my dorm, which meant I got all the tickets for everyone for football and basketball games.

The school I had been attending was more of a commuter college. At North Carolina, I would find that we would be living with each other in a more intense way than I had imagined. Unfortunately, I would end up rubbing some of the people I met the wrong way. For instance, in my dorm room, I hung a big cloth banner that read "Suicidal Tendencies? Join the Army." Join the Army was the name of the album by a group called Suicidal Tendencies. The banner showed a guy with a machine gun, only he had a lot of hair, not like the skin heads. I guess I was in everyone's face from the beginning. An arrogant and cocky New Yorker down South was never a good mix.

That first night, there was a huge party. People packed the lawn drinking beer. The next morning, while walking to my first class, I saw beer cans everywhere. The maintenance crews, not the students, were the ones cleaning up the mess. I thought, "Wow! It's going to be like this every weekend!" Too bad. There were some pretty wild ones, but that was the only party like that one I would see. One of the parties I attended, some guy offered me a shot of Jack Daniels. I turned him down, since I didn't drink hard liquor. My friend whispered to me, "You're in the South. At least put your lips to the glass, so as not to offend him." Another party I got into it a bit when some guys arrived and started taking over the keg. I admit I did some things I'm not proud of today.

Most of the nightlife happened on the main road through town. Some places were legendary, but for the most part it was a typical college town with hangouts, bars, good restaurants and diners.

That first semester, I was still using alcohol and marijuana. I'd have five or six beers, as I'd enjoy the bar scene, and would smoke a joint in the dorm. But nothing excessive. As a sort of initiation, I climbed the water tower tanks twice on a dare with a few of my friends. Why not? But, it was pretty scary climbing the ladder up to the top of the water towers. When we reached the top, we smoked a joint, which seemed the perfect way to celebrate the experience.

An afternoon in the fall of that year is one I will never forget. Something in the atmosphere was special that day. The football team was trounced and still the feeling that everything was perfect was surprisingly not diminished. After the game that afternoon, the band Public Enemy, a black rap/hip hop group from New York was playing at a local club. What else could be better on a Saturday afternoon?

I had to rush at the end of the game to get to the concert on time. A member of the road crew informed me I was late, but the band hadn't started playing yet. I was so relieved not to miss any of the show, as I stood in line for tickets, then found a great spot to watch on the right side of the stage, on top of an elevated stand, which gave me a great view. The club was packed. The opening band was sweating profusely from dancing. When Public Enemy got on stage, the place was electric, the energy so thick you could cut it with a knife. The concert was unbelievable, one of the best concerts I'd ever been to. Everyone there was into it. They played many of my favorites like "Fight the Power."

When the show was over, I walked across the street, back to my room at the dorm, and reflected on the great experience I just had. I also thought about what it must have been like during the time of the Vietnam War, with all of the rebellion on many of the college campuses.

The first time I went home was for the Fall break in October. I was so happy to come home and proud of the way things had gone for me so far. With the Thanksgiving holiday so close to Christmas break, I decided to stay down at school instead of returning home for the holiday.

The day before Thanksgiving, a friend asked me to spend the holiday on his family's farm. I thought it was a good idea at the time, but, as soon as I got there, I could tell I'd made a mistake and wanted to turn around and leave. If only my friends, who were going to a concert at a club close to campus, could swing by and pick me up was all I could think about. But, there was no way to reach them, so I was stuck there. The farm was isolated from the world. When I called home, I learned from my brother that my school had won an exciting game. I couldn't believe I didn't get to see it.

At the farm, there was an invisible fence around the entire property to keep the dog from running away. He'd run up close to the edge, but not too close or he'd get shocked. I felt as trapped on that farm as the dog, even though the family treated me extremely well. I was from New York and had never had such an experience.

They told me the plan was that we'd get up at five in the morning to hunt deer, and we'd be done before the sun was up. I didn't really know what to do under the circumstances. I knew I wasn't going to fire the gun. Even if I wanted to, I didn't have a clue how to use one. The family gave me a practice gun for shooting at targets. All I wanted was to be in bed at that time in the morning. My friend enjoyed shooting. He even carried a hand gun to school. One day at school, he'd dared me to bring the gun he had wrapped in a bag into Hardees, order something and leave. I took him up on his dare and was relieved not to get caught. Being at the farm, though, was a completely new experience. Somehow I was pretty busy, because it ended up that I didn't even do any homework. At night, we drank beer by the camp fire and went to the local night spots. All I knew was that I was glad to go back to my dorm on Sunday.

Christmas break was uneventful. It was nice to be home. Heading back down to Carolina, I was looking forward to another good semester like the first one. I had no clue at all as to the devastation that was about to happen. Everything went okay for the first few weeks of the second semester, until things slowly began to unravel and my mind turned on me.

Some things were changing from the previous semester. My first roommate had pledged and was going to live in the fraternity house, so I would be needing a new roommate. My suite mate, Pete, a psyche major, decided to move in with me. Pete's father was very sick, and Pete was living with the knowledge that his father was going to die soon. We smoked a lot of pot together the first days he lived with me. Smoked, drank, partied. Normally Pete was an upbeat kind of guy, but he was depressed about what he was going through. He tried to kill the feelings he was having with booze and pot. We'd go to different guys' rooms, hang out and just smoke. The different rooms were each like their own subculture. Soon, I began to not feel right. It messed up my mind to be drugged out for so many days straight. Despite smoking all the time, I was still able to maintain my school work, and I didn't cut class once. But, after a few days, I had to stop partying.

Around that time, I somehow lost the kryptonite lock for my $500 Jamis Dakota mountain bike. Or, someone had stolen it. I'd been keeping my bike in my room for a few days, when Pete offered me another lock, a wire one. I should have known it would be easy for someone to clip, but instead, like an idiot, I put the bike out on one of the bike racks by the dorm, securing it with the wire lock. The next morning, I went outside, ready to go to class and couldn't find my bike anywhere. I should have known that all anyone would need was a pair of clippers.

I was very, very upset: "I can't believe I lost my bicycle! This is serious. This is serious." I'd never been violated like that before going to North Carolina. I got really angry and kept ranting about it, especially because I was used to being the one in the role of the perpetrator. Pete didn't seem too upset for me and kept saying I shouldn't worry so much about it. I grew suspicious that he had something to do with the loss of my bike and began to believe I'd been set up to have my bike stolen. After all, he was the one that gave me the weak lock in the first place. But, I never confronted anyone, and Pete was gone soon after that.

Pete left to be with his father, who died a couple of weeks into the second semester. Pete never came back to school, so I had my own room. My other suite mate was also alone, since Pete had been his first roommate, and he never got another one.

My uncle William, my mother's brother, offered to pay for a new bike for me, but I said, "No." I didn't want to get set up again and have another bike stolen. I didn't want him to spend the money on such an expensive bike, either. But, then I had to walk to class, walk into town, instead of riding my bicycle. Now it took forever to get to class, where before I could breeze there in one minute, put the lock on and go right into the classroom. I should have let my uncle buy me a new bike, but I was too certain that it too would be stolen. Losing my bicycle was the first major incident that led to my downfall. The real paranoia began then. It was the beginning of the bad times.

My second semester transcripts showed that I was below a 2.0. I was feeling a lot of pressure. Before attending North Carolina, I had no problem with concentration. My social life was so busy, I figured that that was why I was having a difficult time keeping my mind on studies. I'd even try to work in the study lounge at the dorm, but I couldn't concentrate even there. So many thoughts were going on, I couldn't focus, especially if I was studying something I didn't care about. Even so, I maintained perfect attendance, always did my assignments and participated in class. My lack of concentration could have been an indication of the troubles to come, but at the time I didn't connect any of the dots.

Early in that second semester, I saw a concert with Sick of It All at a club the next town away. I was excited, because they were one of the most popular New York hardcore sort of heavy metal bands.

My friend, John, and I moshed and slam danced. It was a real bonding experience for us. That night, the slam dancing really got violent, but we held our own. Mosh pits and slam dancing are now mainstream, but they weren't back then. Slam dancing's always been about showing how tough you are.

Coming home from the concert, we filled the car up with gas, and I forgot to put the gas cap back on. When we got back to the dorm, we were still all psyched up from the concert, but, Joe, the person we borrowed the car from was pissed off about his gas cap. So, I gave him the money for it. The three of us were pretty good friends. The first time I climbed the water tower was with Joe.

Towards the end of February, the beginning of March, my phone began ringing all hours of the day and night. Whoever was on the other end would hang up as soon as I answered. I guess I'd made some enemies over the first semester, being a little violent, a little arrogant. I was an obnoxious New Yorker kind of guy. People saw me that way from the beginning. But, I was proud to say I was from New York, a big city. I didn't mind bragging. I didn't let people's reactions bother me. In fact, I did some provoking. I challenged people and yelled at people. I was always proud of being tough. The macho thing. I don't think I actually ever got into a fist fight at North Carolina. I was just a hothead. For instance, one time a few of us got a bunch of beers for a party and a bag of ice to keep them chilled. Well, I took the bag of ice, went into the dorm bathroom and violently smashed the bag in the tub. My friends were screaming, "Oh, my God!" And I just said, "So what?"

A couple of weeks after the phone calls started, I began to feel like both people I knew and didn't know so well were following me everywhere. The first time I had the feeling of being watched I'd just walked out of a restaurant, and while I was gazing at the random people walking around, I began to wonder if I was a target. Soon, I began feeling like people were following me to class. I couldn't put a finger on it, but when I looked behind me, the same people were there. Or I'd be sitting in class and would swear people were looking through the door straight at me and then pulling back. Same thing in the cafeteria. I was becoming extremely distracted. Was I imagining it all? In the dorm there was a TV room, like a lounge, and I was watching North Carolina play in the NCAA tournament. Somebody opened the door, looked at me, closed the door and left.

There was no proof, but I honestly felt like I was being set up. Now it's embarrassing to say this, but then it felt so real. Now, even if all this were happening, I wouldn't let it bother me at all. Then, I was so inexperienced; I didn't know what the hell was going on. Everything had changed, and I was messed up. As I walked the campus, I was often out of breath from being so emotionally distressed.

In March, I came home for spring break and got help I needed for my Spanish class. My parents arranged for a tutor to come to the house every day. But, I was so messed up I couldn't concentrate. All semester, I'd been struggling academically. My lack of concentration wasn't the tutor's fault. I was feeling bad mentally and emotionally, because I wasn't doing well in school, and there wasn't anything he could do about it, except help me a little with my assignments. The pressure of academic and social life was breaking me down. More and more people seemed to be taking offense at me.

On the way back down to school, I told myself the next spring break I was going to Florida and party, have the real college experience of my dreams instead of coming home. Unfortunately, by next Spring I would be caught up in the nightmare of hospitalizations. On that trip back down to school, things began to quickly unravel.

CHAPTER THREE

Back at school, I couldn't think clearly at all. The hang up calls intensified. It seemed like everywhere I went, people were following me. Finally, I couldn't eat in the cafeteria. Across the street from my dorm, there was a little shopping center. Everyday, I went to a tiny cafe there and ordered the same thing. I was trying to find a place where I could feel safe, where people wouldn't know where I was. Ordering the same thing every day seemed to give me some comfort. But the money from eating out all the time was adding up.

In order to have the calls and the constant surveillance stop, I believed I needed to change dorms until the end of the school year, and then just go home for the summer. Then everything would begin to be okay again.

A room in a new dorm would be ready in a week, so I stayed at a motel where I'd always stayed whenever I came down with my dad and uncle. Then, for a couple of days, I stayed at the home of friends of my parents. But I couldn't sleep there because the radiator kept banging. I was carrying all the clothes I owned up and down the streets. Despite everything, I was still maintaining perfect attendance.

Everything was okay for a few days after I moved into the second dorm. Then, all of a sudden the phone calls started up again. And the following came again. I knew the phone calls were real, because I heard the phone ring and the person on the other end hang up. Being followed was something I couldn't prove, though I believed the people following me came from the first dorm. Everything that was happening felt weird and got me all messed up.

Sometime in April, I came back home to escape my torment by getting into a new environment. At that point, my parents knew I was messed up, but what could they do? I'd never had psychiatric treatment. I made my rounds visiting friends and was in the face of all the ones who were still living at home, going to the local school, drinking, doing drugs. I went around with my bad attitude, "I'm going to North Carolina." On the surface it did look like I was doing well. I was cursing. "F" this and "F" that. I was angry at the world. It was a full fledge panic time.

My paranoia had followed me home. I was sure everyone was thinking I was such a bad guy because of the violence, that I was an outcast of society as a result. I wasn't sure what was happening. Without thinking, I decided to shave my head. My friend Joe shaved his, so I did, too. It was the worst possible time to do something like that. Now I looked like a skin head, like I was a really violent and bad person. I went to the movies with my brother and a friend of his and left halfway through, because I wasn't feeling well. As I waited outside, I was sure people were talking about me, especially now with my skinhead haircut and my black "Members Only" jacket. "There he is, the tough guy. Don't mess around with him." My paranoia was beginning to consume me.

On the plane on the way back down to school, I broke down crying, feeling that I shouldn't have done such violent things my whole life. I was feeling really messed up about it. I never got into a fight at North Carolina, but before that I'd gotten into a lot of fights. I was always arrogant, bragging I could fight anybody, taking anybody on and acting with no direction. The feeling of being brainwashed grew as I anticipated returning to school, and I wasn't thinking clearly. Now, I believed my life was in danger, and the paranoia was constant. I had no idea what was going on with my mind.

My arrogance was getting worse. I returned to campus, head shaved and wearing a baseball cap with the words, "North Carolina Alumni." Very inappropriate. And I began wearing my black "Members Only" jacket all the time. People had to be saying, "Hey, we're getting annoyed with how this guy acts." All I wanted was to be tough and mean, because that was how I was feeling inside. As soon as I was back on campus, the calls and the following resumed. I began to increasingly worry that I was in physical danger, maybe because of my own violence. The hat was driving everyone crazy, including me.

Soon after returning to school, I was sitting outside by the bookstore, with my alumni cap on to hide my shaved head, feeling, "Oh my God, people are after me." A guy I knew from my first dorm, a friend of a big weight lifter, walked up to me. While I was asking him how his friend was doing, he pulled the cap off to show my shaved head to his girlfriend. Suddenly, I felt like the whole world was either trying to put me away or kill me. My whole life I had defended myself to the death, but at this point I was so scared that my life was in danger that I finally knew what it felt like to be a victim. I felt too threatened to defend myself; if I did anything, I would be in more danger. I believed my paranoia, worry and fear were deserved, because of some of the things I had done in the past. I was a victim because my past made me one.

My thinking was less and less clear, as I tried to figure out what was happening to me. Now I was certain I was being set up, that people were brainwashing me in order to get me to leave school. People were tired of my hat and my skin head, my beer drinking and being loud, and my arrogant, cocky attitude. I was getting on their nerves. There was no part of me that I felt could handle what was going on. I was living in such a different environment than what I was used to that everything that happened felt like a new experience.

At the peak of being messed up, I made plans to study for a final exam with a girl from my first dorm. But I had to stand her up. I was certain being with me would put her in danger, since I was in so much danger myself from being a target.

Finally, I called home and told my parents how people were following me, how I was getting crazy phone calls and never felt well. My father and both uncles came down on the next plane and stayed at the motel to help me get through the end of the semester. I stayed with them.

On April 30, I took my last final, which was Spanish. In the middle of the final, the feeling that people were looking at me grew more and more intense. So, I went up to the teacher and told her I wasn't feeling well and left. A couple of days later, I called her to try to explain. We planned to have a make up final, but it never happened, and I ended up with a C- for the semester, instead of a B.

Finally, the semester was over, and I hoped the nightmare was over, too. In reality, my problems were only beginning.

I felt safer being in New York, no longer in a strange place like North Carolina. I was still out of control, but not as much.

As soon as I got home, my parents took me to see a psychiatrist a couple of times, but I was too against getting that kind of help and too angry about being there to get anything out of therapy. "I don't need help. What do I need help for?"

I was home for a couple of days and was listening to mostly thrash metal and a little Hardcore. The music was anti social, which was how I was feeling. Hardcore lyrics was for real life on the streets. Thrash metal, which I usually preferred, was a blue collar thing. Some of it had to do with Satan. I didn't believe in the devil, but I did listen to the music. Hardcore was for skin heads and was also antisocial. The lyrics were about real life on the streets. Music can have an influence on a person's life, turn them in a different direction.

If I had been left alone for a few days, I might have been able to recover from the semester. Some old friends contacted me and it seemed right away I was out pounding the beers at night, sometimes even during the day. I got right back into the wild life, that I would rather not have had for a few days, so I could have gotten myself together. Instead, I got back into the old scene.

I began to work for my brother's record label, mostly at a computer doing some easy stuff like putting addresses on the mailing lists, calling bands, calling radio stations to make sure they were playing certain songs. I'd tell them that a certain song would be good for their station. I'd only worked one job before, so I thought it was okay to spend a couple of hours there and then go home or hang out around the street. I would hang around the military recruiting center across from my brother's office. There was a strip joint on the street, too, but I didn't go in there. It wouldn't have reflected well on my brother. One day, while I was at work, I decided to go across the street to the deli and have a couple beers. I found myself guzzling it down and wondering what I was doing in the middle of a day having a beer? My lack of responsibility was caused more from being messed up mentally than from lack of job experience.

I ended up spending more and more time at the military recruiting center and was probably pretty annoying to them. I talked at length with the Air Force recruiter, trying to find out what I'd be doing if I joined up. The Army recruiters were encouraging me to join, but I told them I wasn't sure if I wanted to. I took tests for the Army and talked with the Air Force recruiter, all of which led nowhere. I thought I was carrying on the conversation just fine, but I didn't realize how mentally messed up I was. I kept changing my mind about what I wanted to do. Maybe I'd take a year off from school, join the military, then go back to school. Should I even go back to school in the fall? At this point, I still felt I was okay, I was still sane. I wasn't yet in actual trouble. I wasn't in a hospital yet.

A friend of the family worked helping to repair things inside and out of my family's house. On my own, I ended up helping him quite a bit, mostly screwing in the shutters, because I decided I now wanted to be known as a blue collar worker.

People knew I was on the wrong track. My parents knew, but they couldn't do anything, because I didn't actually do anything wrong. I refused to go to the psychiatrist, because I didn't want anyone messing with my head. My parents kept telling me the doctor would put me on medication that would help me, but I was rebellious. I hadn't initiated the visits and felt there was a stigma attached to me now that I'd seen a psychiatrist.

Once, when I was being picked up at the psychiatric center, I overheard someone talking about Generation X, and I thought to myself: "Yep, none of us are free." My generation was a disaster. So many of my generation got locked up, lost their freedom, got in trouble, messed up in school and got involved with drugs. Generation

X. It seemed so many of my heroes either ended up behind bars or in hospitals. A certain kind of intelligence was missing to help with making better decisions. If I'd known what I know now, I would have done better. But I didn't have the knowledge to change things. I didn't realize what I was getting myself into or how to get out of situations. I just didn't know how to act.

I was born in 1969, when the Vietnam War was still going strong. The sixties were about drugs. Too many drugs, too much war, not enough respect for the soldiers who were returning. My mother loved the fifties. She could talk for hours about the fifties, which I couldn't relate to at all. We are the generation without freedom. A lot of people ended up messed up, friends as well as heroes. It happened to them, then it happened to me.

Though I hadn't consulted a guidance counselor, I thought I needed two classes to return to North Carolina in the fall, should I want to go back. So I registered for a couple of make-up classes at a local New York college. Suddenly, instead of the feeling of being followed everywhere, I felt like I was a star, that everyone was interested in me because I was attending such a prestigious school. The first day, I dropped a math class because it seemed too hard for me. But I continued with two others, met some new people and managed to function all right.

Being home, though, began to feel like a distraction and on impulse I decided to drive to North Carolina to start fresh and attend the second semester of summer school there. I was now too uncomfortable in New York and feeling like I was getting too much attention at school there.

One day I announced my decision and the next day I was on the road back down to North Carolina. My parents couldn't stop me. I was on a dangerous path. This time, I drove the blue Pontiac Sunbird my parents got me when I turned sixteen. If that car could talk, I'd be in a lot of trouble.

My trip was a disaster. I found myself getting lost, and I got a speeding ticket in Virginia. When I arrived, I stayed at the usual motel. My father and uncle followed me down to help me get through everything and arranged for an acquaintance, Eddie, to get me an apartment. He would turn out to be the greatest friend anyone could ask for. Even so, I was ungrateful, reckless and sometimes nasty to my family. They did their best, but I was out of control.

With three withdrawals from summer school in New York, I signed up for two classes at North Carolina. I did very well in one, but was failing in the other. Overall, I was still messed up.

My paranoia kicked in big time again. Despite my mental turmoil, I lasted a couple of weeks, taking classes in the morning, lifting weights and playing basketball in the afternoons, which I enjoyed. But my fears intensified. As much as I wanted to go home, I was afraid to drive or fly.

On July 14, I called home and told my parents I didn't know what to do. I was depressed, unhappy and extremely confused. Things weren't horrible, but I felt lost. Finally, I thought maybe I could get some kind of treatment, because I could see how I was all over the place with driving down to North Carolina, dropping out of classes, doing poorly in the ones I was taking. It wasn't like I was hearing voices. I was just scattered and looking for direction.

CHAPTER FOUR

After pulling into the parking lot of the Trauma Center, I sat in my car for a little while, debating whether or not to go in. Deep down I knew I had to get help. As soon as I could after entering the building, I voiced out loud for the first time my feelings of wanting to kill myself. When the medical personnel suddenly called the police, I couldn't figure out what I had done to anyone. Then, standing outside the psychiatric unit, a police officer on either side of me, I wondered what had I done to myself? I had to finish summer school. If I'd realized what I was getting myself into by going to the Trauma Center, had known that I was going to be admitted immediately, I would have never sought help there. I could have received help outside the hospital. As soon as the last door was locked behind me, the realization sunk in that I would be imprisoned for a while. I'd made a big mistake. "Boy, did I screw up now," was all I could think.

I was labeled paranoid schizophrenic. They had to label me something. I don't know if I have schizophrenia. That's a tough one to say. There I was acquiring a label before I was actually admitted and after seeing a psychiatrist only twice in my life, and never having been on medication. I was a junior, finishing my junior year at a major school and all of a sudden I was in a mental hospital. It was tough. I had no idea what they were going to do with me. Never had I been in such a situation.

I suspected my paranoia came from not being able to adjust to the advancements I'd made by attending the school of my dreams. I'd reached such a high goal, but I hadn't grown up enough to be able to handle the success. The paranoia didn't seem severe enough to cause me to be admitted to a psychiatric hospital. I should have taken my parents' advice and seen a psychiatrist. That was what I had needed to do. If I'd been put on medication while being home during the summer, I would have been okay and nothing so drastic as being committed to a psych ward would have happened. I just didn't accept my parents' advice. Who me? I didn't need anyone's help. Now things had escalated to the point I wanted to kill myself.

I had to wonder that, if I hadn't gone to North Carolina, my breakdown might not have happened. If I had stayed at home in New York, I might have coped with things better, being in familiar surroundings. In the end, it was impossible to know what would have actually happened to me. Maybe at home I would have gotten into trouble with the law?

I felt completely alone in the locked ward with all the others. As soon as I could, I called my parents to tell them what happened. They kept saying over and over, "This is not a punishment. The doctors are only trying to help you." But the hospital was a horrible place, and it felt like I was being punished.

The first meal there I found myself thinking obsessively: "Society doesn't want me any more. What do I have left to contribute to society? Nothing. People want me to kill myself. I've got to end it all." I hid a plastic knife and brought it back to the room, sat on my bed and began scraping my arm. It wasn't an act of suicide, but more of a cry for help. A plastic knife- what was that going to do? I still have a bad scar on my wrist from those feelings of desperation.

I was surprised that I was left alone in my room with no doctors to help me or prevent me from killing myself, when I'd told them that I'd wanted to commit suicide. They had committed me, put me in the locked unit to prevent me from following through, but then just left me alone. That wasn't right. Obviously, I'd set myself up, when only that morning I'd been heading to town. I kept thinking over and over, "Boy did I make a mistake seeking help there."

Finally, one of the mental health workers walked into my room, grabbed the knife and said, "You can't be doing this!" I was glad to hand over the knife. I didn't really want to kill myself. I was trying to get their attention. I didn't know what was going on or what to expect, and I just wanted some attention. But I didn't get any, despite my extreme efforts. Unfortunately, the fact that I had scraped my wrist for sure didn't help me get out of there any sooner. As the reality that I had been committed sunk in, I kept thinking, "I'm out of society now, and people want me to kill myself." Clearly I was mentally unstable, but I didn't realize how much.

Everyday routines of the hospital took over: wake up, blood pressure monitoring first thing, then pills, eat breakfast. Every morning I ordered chocolate milk, the highlight of the day. After breakfast, I'd go back to sleep in my unmade bed. I tried to sleep as much as I could. Otherwise, I watched TV, walked around outside, attended meetings. The doctor said I was good at leading the meetings, which made my parents happy. But I didn't care. I only cared about getting out of there. Once in a while, I bummed a cigarette from someone. I wasn't a smoker, but I said, "What the hell?" I wasn't in the alcohol or drug treatment programs, so I didn't go to those meetings.

It was horrible being locked in all day. The routine was abnormal. Who lived like that? And so I began to feel abnormal myself. I went from going to North Carolina to this place? What had I done to myself, was all I could think about? Sleep was difficult. One night a nurse asked me if I was hearing voices. I wasn't, but for some reason I said, "Yes." She made a note of it.

After a couple of days, I went to a hearing to determine how much more time I had to stay. The hospital had their own little court. I thought for sure my lawyer would get me out. When I got on the stand, I made my case. I told them I didn't know what I was getting myself into when I went there for help. But my explanations weren't good enough. The judge said I had to be in there for another sixty days, when I would have another hearing to determine if I could leave. So there was no guarantee that I would get out even after sixty days. That was a shock. I pleaded with the judge to let me go back to New York, but he said, "Absolutely no." I'd sure gotten myself into a tough bind.

My mother, who never flies, flew down to see me. I had a calendar and marked the days off until I could leave. I never began to feel any better during the whole time there. Adjusting to such a different life was impossible.

Our unit had relatively few patients. A few days after my arrival, a blonde named Karen was admitted. I'd walk by her room and she'd be sitting on her bed with her head low, really depressed. Her sister, who visited her all the time, was a student at North Carolina. Really good looking. Another patient was twenty-seven and played professional football. What was he doing there, I wondered? He had several girls visiting him. Another fellow was in the Marines and would let me borrow his weights. When he got out of the hospital, he planned to return to the Marines. I asked him how he thought he could go back after being hospitalized, and he said he wasn't going to tell them. I doubted he could get away with that. One guy, who was twenty-four, was bipolar. He loved watching college football on Saturdays. They all seemed pretty normal, and I could relate to them somewhat. But, most of the other patients were pretty sick and just walked around all the time in a daze.

I was aware of when the fall semester began. Whenever I was out walking on campus as an outing, I'd recognize some classmate and kept thinking that it couldn't be true that I was not one of them going to classes. I wanted so badly to be in school. One Saturday, one of the mental health workers snuck me into a football game. I watched the team kick a field goal, and that made me feel even worse that I wasn't a student enjoying myself. At the game, I saw someone I knew and said, "Hello," which was brutal.

The feeling of being followed had disappeared. Why would anyone want to follow me into a place like that? Why would anyone want to bother with me now at all? I believed they got what they wanted- they got rid of the hotheaded New Yorker. I felt much better that the calls and following weren't happening anymore, but at the same time I felt less important. Did anyone even care about me anymore? Not that I wanted the calls and the following to resume.

The depth of my depression about having to stay there was hard to fathom. As the sixty days were coming up, I began to beg my parents to get me out, even if it meant I would have to be transferred to a hospital in New York. I couldn't stand being locked up one more day.

Eddie, the man who had helped me get an apartment, began visiting me every single day, mostly during his lunch break or sometimes after work. Eddie worked at the alumni office of North Carolina. Over the years, my dad and uncle had given a lot of money to the school. Eddie took over much of my care when my parents couldn't be there. After I was hospitalized, he drove around trying to find my car. He was the kind of guy who couldn't do enough for people. He was unbelievable. My mom called him all the time. The family couldn't have done without him. Eddie understood that it was incredibly brutal to be in a mental hospital on the campus of the college I was so proud of attending. The depression was huge. Eddie helped me through it, all on his own with nothing to be gained. My family had hardly known him, except through alumni giving, but, whenever anything had to be done, they could do it through him.

As always, when I needed them the most, my dad and uncle came down to stay and help me through the rest of my stay. They were able to get me out of the hospital for six hours each day, with the promise that they would keep me with them at all times. But, if they took me to the movies, I'd find myself leaving halfway through, feeling depressed that I wasn't in school instead. Once when I walked out, I noticed a girl working at the theater was studying during a break. I wanted so much to be studying like her. I kept wishing I could do everything over and differently this time. My parents kept telling me over and over that the hospitalization wasn't a punishment.

During one of our six hour outings, my dad, uncle and I went to a restaurant and saw the football coach. The weights I was borrowing to work out with were small. As a result, I'd lost some of my build and looked pretty weak. I'd always dreamed of walking onto the football team, and here I was face to face with the coach and in horrible physical shape. Everything was a reminder of lost dreams.

I was constantly begging my parents to get me out of the hospital. My impatience was going to cause me to make a big mistake. Because my admittance had been involuntary, I was under the hospital's jurisdiction and had no option but to wait for a hearing after sixty days. When the sixty days were up, I sought another hearing from the judge, who would determine if it was time for me to leave or if I had to spend more time in treatment. The judge ordered me to stay another twenty-four days, the maximum he could ask for. After the twenty-four days, I would be out for good, no matter what. Instead of listening to the judge's advice, I insisted my lawyer fight to get me transferred to a hospital in New York, so I could be close to home and my family could visit every day. I believed I would have really gone crazy if I'd stayed in that environment any longer.

So I was released to my father on September 18. My uncle drove back up to New York with us. We stopped and spent the night in Maryland, stayed at a nice motel and had a wonderful meal, which should have been a real treat. But all I could think of was that I wasn't free, that I was in for more hard times, so how could I enjoy any of it? I had wanted to be released from the New York hospital in seventy-two hours, which was an option, if the staff approved, but my mother said I should stick with the whole program and get well. If I would go through with it, they would let me come back home. Home seemed so much more important to me now, especially compared to all I had been through, that I decided to comply.

The mistake I made was not going ahead with the extra twenty-four days in North Carolina and just having it all over with. When Dwight Gooden was arrested for drugs, he could have spent five years in rehab and treatment, but he wouldn't have been free. Or he could go to jail for seven months. He chose to be free after seven months. I understood his choice.

The agreement with the judge was that I'd be driven straight to the hospital in New York. As we turned onto the grounds, I thought to myself, "This place looks even more horrible." At least in North Carolina I was surrounded by the campus, which was full of life and activity. This place looked dreary, like from a Dickens novel. The awful weather didn't help the impression. After parking the car and getting my things out of the trunk, we walked through the bleak halls to the unit, where they gave me a physical. There I was, starting all over again at another hospital.

CHAPTER FIVE

The first night at the hospital in New York, I slept with a mental health worker sitting by my bed. Since it was my first night there, they might have been concerned that I could do harm to myself. Being heavily medicated, I didn't think much of it.

After a few days, when I was not as heavily sedated as when they tried to acclimate me on arrival, I realized this hospital was one of the worst places imaginable. As winter approached and the trees lost their leaves, the grounds grew bleaker and bleaker with the bare branches and brown soggy leaves on the ground. The gloomy environment matched how I was feeling. The weather seemed colder than normal. Still, it helped to walk the grounds, one of the privileges we got only if we behaved.

I behaved myself, because I wanted to get out of there, out of the dark hallways and dreary rooms, where we had no freedom and no privacy. I spent the days watching the clock, waiting for visiting hours. A lot of time was passed sleeping on the sofa out in the hall. We weren't allowed in our rooms during the day. They didn't want us vegetating in our rooms, but I would try to sleep on the couch, mostly to get the time to pass quickly. A day seemed like a year.

My parents came every day. My uncle and my brothers came sometimes. My family was great. Most people never had visitors.

When my parents visited, all I could talk about was how unhappy I was. "I've got to get out of here!" Those were my famous words every time they came to see me. The one thing that made me feel better was that I knew I was going back home after sixty days, that I wouldn't be living in an out patient facility, where I'd have to be surrounded by other patients.

My mother would always arrive early to get a good parking place and sit in the car, waiting for visiting hours to start. The medical personnel didn't like her being there all the time. They felt it wasn't good for me, but she thought they were wrong and came every night anyway. Mom was allowed to take me on the grounds, and she'd let me drive in the parking lot. Once, they questioned her about that, and she told them that driving the car helped me feel normal. Mom was annoyed that someone was watching us like that. One night I had a bloody nose, and she ran right over to the hospital. They didn't like that she was there so much, but her motherly instincts were too strong to keep her away.

Once, my second oldest brother brought me a new Slayer cassette, "Seasons in the Abyss." At first I was excited to have it, but then I thought about how I was in the abyss. My brother told me, "You're in the mecca of mental hospitals." I guess he meant I was in the best hospital there was, but I didn't appreciate his comment. It felt like he was knocking me down. I wanted to say, "Thanks a lot! You don't know. You're not here. You're free. You put yourself in Mecca and see how you feel." I felt like he was happy that I was there.

Only five months before, I had been a student at North Carolina, and now I was a mental patient locked up in a hospital, going to groups that held zero interest for me instead of attending my college classes. The men's groups and sports classes, like volleyball, all sucked. It was brutal. The purpose of one of the men's groups was just to hash over what it was like for us being in the hospital. What the heck did they think we were feeling about our "experience"?

The gym class was bearable, since I was an athlete, though volleyball, which we mostly played, wasn't my favorite sport by any means. Once in a while, we could play basketball or ping pong. There wasn't a weight room, but I wouldn't have wanted to lift weights anyway, because I was feeling so down. What if I worked out once, what was that going to do for me? Absolutely nothing was going on on the weekends, so time seemed interminable.

The food wasn't bad. Three meals a day and a snack at night. There was a place to hang out called the Canteen- the hospital's definition of a "party place." Kids would get together and drink soda. I wanted to be in a bar. Everyone had a job and mine was to clean pots and pans for the Canteen. They didn't like how I was doing the job. In one conversation, I told a worker that I'd gone to North Carolina. Even though his response was, "Oh, wow!", I got angry with him because I was so frustrated about how far away from North Carolina I was, scrubbing pots and pans in a mental hospital. There was also a hospital store where they sold candy and newspapers. I'd collect people's money and get them what they needed, a little reminiscent of my job getting tickets for students in the dorm at North Carolina.

Now I was surrounded by people from New York that were sick, instead of being around sick Southerners. Most people walked the halls in a medicated daze. I talked with a guy who wore a New York University cap. He was twenty-eight and this was his eighteenth hospitalization. I was amazed and shocked. Little did I know that I would pretty much equal his numbers.

A Spanish kid from the Bronx was the only person I could really relate to, the only one who could help me get through it. He caused some problems sometimes, but he was actually pretty cool. He was seventeen; I was twenty. He was a street kid, a fighter, and I could relate to him for that reason alone. Even though I grew up in a wealthy area, in the group I'd hung around with you'd have to be pretty tough to be accepted. So, we understood each other, even though he came from the Bronx. He made it easier being there, but then he got out. When he left, I had no one. "Ah, boy. Now I'm really alone." I couldn't relate to anyone there, these were people I never would want to hang around with. So, I didn't want to talk to anybody. I didn't even want to read a magazine. All I wanted was to get out of there.

My social worker was beautiful- like an oasis. I couldn't believe I was lucky enough to be seeing someone like her in there. It was a special treat. I felt like she knew I didn't belong there. She promised to get me released but said I would have to be in an outpatient program, a facility on the grounds. I could stay at home with my parents and go to the program during the day. Already, I wasn't crazy about that idea.

Both hospitalizations were hard to get through, but the one in New York was a brutal, brutal experience. I felt like I was paying my debt to society by being there. If I were on the outside, smoking pot and drinking, I still would have been considered mainstream, instead of being thought of as an outcast of society from being in a psychiatric hospital. I felt if I could get out of there, then I could decide what I wanted to do with my life. Both hospitals failed me, because the experience lowered my self-esteem, which didn't help me cope at all when I got out. I didn't feel comfortable being surrounded by patients that were very sick and had a lot of personal problems. I must have been like them, but I couldn't relate. Losing my freedom, feeling like a prisoner just made me worse instead of well again.

While I was there, the Cincinnati Reds played in the World Series. Pete Rose was in jail at the time. His brother was in the stands wearing a Cincinnati Reds jacket. I thought to myself then that I'd rather be in jail than in a mental hospital, because at least you knew when you were getting out. You could defend yourself. I'd had the same thoughts about Dwight Gooden choosing jail rather than rehab. I completely understood his decision.

After the second semester at North Carolina, when I was really breaking down, I had read in the paper about one of my classmates, a senior and a basketball player, who had legal problems. Months later, when I was an outpatient on the grounds of the hospital, the newspaper showed him holding a basketball, looking forward to the new season. Sad, his season was probably ruined. Hopes dashed, just like mine. It was brutal to realize that, despite his legal problems, at least he was still playing and was going to graduate on time. Generation X. We didn't even have heroes to look up to who weren't also getting into trouble.

The best thing that happened to me while I was there was watching the New York Giants win a big football game. They kicked a field goal in the last seconds to win. One small moment of happiness.

They began easing me out of the hospital. I was able to go home for a couple of hours to celebrate my birthday. I was twenty-one. We had a cake and a low key celebration. A couple of times toward the end of my stay, I was allowed to go see my outside psychiatrist, the one I had hated going to the summer before. Now, I was so talkative with him. I felt I had to get so much out after not having anyone I could relate to in the hospital. I was beginning to taste freedom.

Finally, the day came. I was out of the hospital, November 21, 1990, after sixty days there. The weather was crummy, and I was too depressed from my experience to celebrate. I swore to myself

I was never coming back to any place like that. I kept thinking about the patient who was readmitted eighteen times. How could such a thing be possible? I was so depressed inside those walls. How could I not live as a free person? I believed in freedom above all else. At that point, I had no idea that I would be in and out of mental institutions, with one less admittance than the fellow with the New York University cap.

Unfortunately, hospitalization just made me worse. If, after I'd finished my junior year at North Carolina, I'd come home and relaxed for a few weeks, I probably would have been okay to go back to North Carolina for my senior year. I needed time to throw off the feelings of being followed. The phone calls never happened in New York, so was it all in my imagination? Obviously, I had problems and if I had gone to a psychiatrist and been on medication as soon as I got home for the summer, the hospitalizations could have been prevented. In order to keep the stress off, I probably would have had to take an extra semester to graduate. And it would have had to have been done with a psychiatrist's supervision. So, I left the New York hospital full of regrets.

I'm not saying it was the fault of the doctors, but circumstances led to worse things happening. I'd been so proud of myself going to North Carolina, and then to end up in a psych ward was too much. Before I knew it, I was back doing the same things: hanging around with my high school friends, drinking, smoking weed and a little hard drugs like crack cocaine. I preferred the crack cocaine, because it was an upper. It was just a hanging around thing. I was living at home again. Nothing had changed me. I was happy to get out, but I was back to square one- back into the neighborhood. I wasn't mentally worse than before being admitted. The paranoia was gone, but psychologically my self esteem was so low, and in that way I was even more messed up.

Living at home again wasn't easy, though I was grateful to be able to be there. My older brother was still living at home, and it didn't seem like there was room enough for both of us, even though he had a job and a girlfriend and spent much of his time away. When we were both home, we would be playing our music loud at the same time.

Getting back with old friends, I felt I had gone back down to their level. Going away to college, especially to such a prestigious one, I was a cut above, had made something of myself. Now I was back living my old life with them. I had gotten above their level, but now I'd knocked myself down a notch. It wasn't that I didn't like my friends. I wasn't judging them. I just wanted more for myself than they did. But, at least they were good friends that I could have fun with and hang out with. I didn't say anything to most of them about my hospitalizations, but some of them I told. I was embarrassed, and I felt like I was lower than I was. I was coming from worse than the "lower level"- one of Public Enemy's terms.

Public Enemy was a blue collar type of a group, one of the biggest hip hop groups of all time. Hardcore hip hop. A lot of anger, but also a message. "It Takes a Nation of Millions to Hold Us Back" is the title of one of the biggest hip hop CD's of all time. On the cover of their CD is a picture of themselves in jail standing behind bars. It Takes a Nation of Millions to Hold Us Back. Another CD was called Muse Sick-N-Hour-Mess Age. Clever. Public Enemy is still one of my major influences today.

Chuck D, their lead singer, was someone I really looked up to and was a big influence on me in the nineties, when everything was going wrong with me. He always said he was on the "lower level," meaning he was a man of the people. From the band, Public Enemy's, point of view, the "lower level" was about getting a message to the general population, that the band was on their level and they were a group of the common person. A person who is not of the lower level is someone who has it all, and who doesn't have to deal with everyday situations. But I felt I was lower than the "lower level."

Though I grew up in the suburbs and not the inner city, I had anger which came from setbacks like the broken leg. I didn't grow up very happy. I don't know why. I was always into the antisocial music, basically since age twelve or thirteen. The drug use maybe put me on edge when I was a junior or senior in high school. But what knocked me down a whole level were the hospitals. I was always able to be an antisocial person, but I was able to conform as well through academics and athletics.

The initial agreement with my social worker was that, after getting out of the hospital, I would go to an outpatient day program on the hospital grounds. My mother drove me there in the morning and then picked me up at the end of the day. All I did while in the program was lie on the couch and try to sleep the day away. The doctors and mental health workers monitored our every move. I felt like a rat in a cage. Sometimes, I'd walk to the hospital store, but the halls were so dreary I became more depressed. I put on a good performance, so that they would hopefully find no more reasons for me to be there. How was I supposed to be getting better? The best part of the day was getting out of there. At least I was able to come home at night.

While there, I read in the newspaper about one of the basketball players from North Carolina, who had gotten in trouble with the law. "At least," I thought to myself, "he is still in a better position than I am. The team had made the final four that year. Something good was happening for him, despite his problems." Nothing like that could be said about my situation.

After a week, I couldn't take being in the day program anymore and convinced my mother that they couldn't keep me there, that I was free now. I wasn't locked in anymore. Why did I have to keep going? I didn't need it. I told my parents I would do something- go back to school. At that point, I wouldn't have been able to work. So, I was released from the program. I was dangerous but I was free. Everything was so messed up with my life, though, that I wasn't even that happy about being free.

Being out and home felt strange. The trouble now became, what was I going to do with my life? What was I going to do with myself? I couldn't imagine where I could go from where I'd just been. Should I go back to school? Back to North Carolina? I felt like I had unfinished business there. I still wanted to graduate from there. My parents quickly put an end to that option. My mom said the only way I could go back down south to school would be if my father went down with me like a shadow. He would have willingly, but I didn't want to do that. It took me a while to get over the idea of not being able to go down to North Carolina, of never having the feeling again of being on a pedestal for such an achievement. And then it took ten years to completely get over not graduating from there.

For the next month I worked out, jogging and lifting weights. In January, I went back to school for a winter session course- a crash two week course in history between fall and spring semesters.

I'd been recovering only a month and wasn't yet back to myself, when I saw two brothers that I'd known from high school at registration. When I said, "Hi, how are you?" one asked. "Hey, break any beer bottles lately?" All of a sudden, I was the one being made an example of. I was always making others the example for not measuring up. The tables had turned on me. At least when I was at North Carolina, I had that prestige to back me up. Now I was all in shambles: at a local school close to home (even though it was a good one), going from the university to North Carolina psychiatric hospital to a New York psychiatric hospital, only out about a month, having missed a full semester at school. The summer before I hadn't completed any classes. Dropped five that summer. I used to make fun of people who transferred from one not so good school to another not so good school- not so good according to my standards- and here I was transferring from a mental hospital.

It was freezing out. I couldn't fight him over the comment about the beer bottles. I already felt much lower and more sensitive than in the past, and his comments just made me feel worse. I'd known him for years. None of my friends knew what I'd gone through, and I was really paranoid about people finding out. I would have hated for people to know, but I realized I would have to begin seeing people and explain some humiliating things to them. I just wasn't prepared.

Chapter Six

All my life, I had high standards. I wanted to overachieve. I wanted to be respected. I always wanted to persevere. "Perseverance" was the name of a CD from a hardcore heavy metal band named Hatebreed. I used that word to define myself because of that CD.

Adjustment to life after all I'd been through was a little difficult. But, I managed to get by in the history class, and then in the spring I enrolled in an art history class. A girl I knew from high school was in that class, and she was set to graduate on time. I was jealous that she was nearly finished and got it in my mind that I wanted to graduate as soon as possible, and I didn't care from where. I felt downtrodden as I realized just how many credits I lost by my parents' and somewhat my decision that I shouldn't go back down to North Carolina to graduate. Of course I understood why it was best to finish at a local school, but I felt I still had unfinished business at North Carolina. Still, it was frustrating to have so much of my work not count.

I began searching for the school that would accept the most credits from all I had taken. One local school surprised me by accepting nearly all my credits, many more than any other school, which would enable me to graduate quicker. But I would have to major in Criminal Justice or Journalism in order for all the credits to count.

I figured down the road, Criminal Justice would help me more. So I decided to go ahead and major in Criminal Justice, anything just to get a degree and move on with my life. But it was a real letdown going to a local school rather than a great school like North Carolina. Some friends didn't understand my depression about that. "Hey, so what?" They didn't have a clue.

So I was at my fourth school. It took me two years to graduate. While there, I did some extracurricular activities such as intramural softball and basketball. I was also a DJ at the campus radio station. My brother got me a job at an athletic shoe store. Unfortunately, I had some trouble with the job. I couldn't find shoes in the stock room, had trouble getting apparel from high off the wall, and it was difficult for me to measure shoe sizes. Even though I worked only one or two days a week, I couldn't adjust to the job for some reason. The hospitalizations had undermined my confidence, and so I had a hard time adjusting to work and sticking with things.

In one of my Criminal Justice classes, I asked my favorite professor if it was possible for someone who'd been in rehab to get a job in the field. A couple of days later, I was in his office and he asked me the reason for my question. When I told him what I'd been through, he said there was still a pretty good chance, which was encouraging.

In June of the summer after my release from the New York hospital, I called a local radio station and got a job as an intern. Training for the station was a couple of days a week. I learned how to engineer a show, and eventually had my own show on Saturday nights, in which I played soft music- oldies, something I couldn't have cared less about. I paid the station to let me do a Death Metal show, which was about really fast guitars and drums- a fast heavy metal and a lot of Satanic stuff- once a week for a couple of months. Work at the radio station lasted three years. Music was such an important part of my life that it gave me the confidence I needed to keep that job. But finally I left, because I didn't really like working there. My parents wanted me to stay, but I had already found a job at a record store.

My social life remained the same. I was still drinking and doing drugs with mainly two of my friends. Even during the week I'd be using. One of my friends was a big drinker. The other drank a lot and also did drugs. I was still a bit violent and got into some scrapes in the bars.

I continued seeing the same psychiatrist twice a week and then it was reduced to once a week for the next five years. He knew about my drinking, but I never told him about smoking marijuana. We mostly spent time talking about sports, North Carolina, music, hanging out at the bars, girls- all the things I was interested in. We had a very good relationship.

I graduated with the class in May 1993, even though I had to finish a couple of classes in the summer and actually only qualified to graduate in August. The ceremony itself was pretty nice, though I kept thinking about the fact that I wasn't graduating from North Carolina and what a loss that was for me. It seems crazy to mention it all the time, but it was such a magical school.

After graduation, I asked myself, what did I want to do with my life? I realized I wanted to go into acting, because I wanted to make it big. I'd majored in radio/television and motion pictures, so I always had the love for the camera and the lights. I wanted to make it big and put all my demons behind me. I took a two week commercial crash course in how to succeed in commercials. Before that course, I'd taken a one on one acting class at the Y. I discovered I liked being under the bright lights.

For a few dollars, I bought a mailing list and found a woman named Donna, who was able help organize me sending out headshot fliers. She was a great source for mailing stickers to all the different casting directors. We went to lunch, and she gave me some good information and convinced me to join the union AFTRA, the American Federation of Television and Radio Artists. She also felt I had a good chance to make it. I asked my parents if they could pay for her services, mailing out resumes and headshots to agents and casting directors, and they agreed. Donna got me a lot of good work in '94 and '95.

Acting was so much fun, and I enjoyed it a lot more than radio, because it was far more exciting. Psychologically, I was still not a hundred percent. Sometimes I had problems with a little paranoia, but I was able to get by. I was twice each on the soap operas Guiding Light and As the World Turns. With Guiding Light, we filmed the end of one episode and the beginning of another, so I got paid for a couple of episodes and made a couple of hundred dollars. Another time on Guiding Light, I played a gang member, but never was on camera as it turned out. On As the World Turns, I played a criminal, handcuffed and walking through a police station. Basically, background work.

I was typecast as a criminal most of the time. My Criminal Justice degree and my wild hair both contributed. Most of the roles I played were antisocial in nature. Once, though, for the soap opera Another World, I auditioned for the role of a doctor. I was so excited about that audition.

Donna was also able to get me on USA Up All Night, Saturday Night Live and some promotional work for a Phil Donohue Show episode. Again, on the Phil Donohue promotion, I was a criminal. I wore my Slayer shirt and a leather vest, and they filmed me running away after stealing a purse from a lady, then getting caught on the top of a building and handing over the purse with my hands up. The cops were shown walking away after making the arrest.

I was in movies that never made it to the big screen, and did lots of jobs for free, because I enjoyed acting so much. I was gaining a lot of confidence and making up for the confidence I lost by not finishing at North Carolina. Donna really produced for me and got me some great work.

Being on Saturday Night Live was great. We rehearsed for a couple of hours on a Friday, then had to be at the studio at one o'clock on Saturday afternoon and stay until the show ended, a good twelve hours. We were playing barbarians in a skit with Chevy Chase. I had just cut my hair, so they gave me a wig. The other actors also wore wigs. We were dressed in barbarian costumes and boots, and had lots of face paint. We stood at the bottom of a staircase. It was a skit about the movie Braveheart. Whenever anyone said the word, "Braveheart," we had to cheer like barbarians. The skit was funny, and I was on a lot.

But I walked out on a few acting jobs, and that wasn't a good thing. I was still unstable at times. Once I had a job on As the World Turns, and I had my mother call them the night before and cancel. I didn't want to be on television in a compromising position. Another time, I had a job on Guiding Light and was already at the studio, when I suddenly left because I was feeling paranoid. I just felt uncomfortable, and a place like that shouldn't have made anyone feel that way. One of the greatest accomplishments is to get on a soap opera. I also left in the middle of filming a commercial. I had a job on Miracle on 34th Street, but that required getting up at six in the morning and working until seven at night. Back then, I had trouble waking up early. I was able to make it the first day, but the second day I overslept and got there late, and they told me to leave.

In June of 1994, I quit my job at the record store, where I'd been working two nine-hour shifts a week, which enabled me to keep the acting going. I quit because of a fight I'd gotten into. I was always hanging out in bars, and there was also a strip club I would frequent. One night, I was trying to pick up a dancer there, showing her my radio card to impress her that I was a disc jockey, when she said she was already going out with the owner of the club. I said I thought he was already going out with another one of the girls. Actually, he probably went out with all of them.

The owner called me into his back room to ball me out. I tried to make an excuse, but he punched me in the face, and I was thrown back into the wall. So then I challenged him when I got outside. But he had several bouncers, especially one really big guy, so I came out on the losing end. I was really bent out of shape over the incident, so much so that the frustration carried over and I quit my job at the record store because of it. My parents were really upset, but what could they do?

With more time on my hands, I asked Donna if she could get me working as an actor full time. Was there anything for me to do? She said there was a semester course at a prestigious local acting school. I started the course in September of '94. Completed the semester. Was fine. My classmates were cool. I enjoyed it. I liked the attention and the fun of being in the spotlight, being a star. I liked the acting and the general atmosphere. It was just a lot of fun. Acting classes were Tuesdays, Wednesdays and Thursdays, and I'd stay with my brother and uncle in Manhattan. Acting class in the evening and hung around my brother's apartment during the day. I was still going to the gym and working out.

I hung around with a lot of friends who were in bands and went to their shows. We used to go slam dancing and we were violent. We'd rule the mosh pit. It was crazy stuff. Crazy stuff. We'd go to shows. There was a place in Westchester, another in Brooklyn. The mosh pits were really violent. The music didn't create the anger, but it did contribute to it.

My boss at the record store let me come back to work on Saturdays and Sundays. That was in October of 1994.

Meanwhile, after going through a series of classes together, a group of us at the acting school decided to do an intensive course together, so we arranged a spring semester schedule. At first I thought, no I shouldn't, but then changed my mind, which was a mistake on my part. At the time, I was still not 100% psychologically. I was always quitting things when I didn't feel like doing something. Three weeks into the spring semester, we were doing a skit where I was chasing this guy and he threw a chair at me. I got upset about it, took it too seriously, walked out and never came back.

I wasn't doing all that well since leaving the hospital in New York. I was too involved with drinking and drugs. Obviously, I didn't want the hospitalizations to happen again, but I wasn't doing that well to prevent it. I reverted back to the old self with the drinking and the drugs and quitting my job. Some things were good and some things weren't during those five years. The acting was going well. I was getting jobs. But then I left the acting school. I quit the radio station; I quit the job at the record store. I'd leave early from work and generally not act too responsibly. Even with the acting, I'd left a couple of those good jobs. I was worse in between than I realized. Sometimes I would get panic attacks and call my mother that I was coming home. She'd always tell me to try to stay. The people at the record store were very understanding.

I had low self esteem. A lot of my life revolved around going to bars and drinking. I enjoyed it, but it wasn't a healthy lifestyle physically or mentally. To my mind, that was the effect that the hospitalizations had had on me. The low self esteem caused me to go back with my old friends, work here and there, and quit things. I was quitting a lot of things because my confidence level wasn't as it should have been like when I was going to North Carolina. Not that I didn't have challenges at North Carolina, but I stuck things out and didn't quit then. I didn't really care that I was living an unhealthy lifestyle. It didn't bother me.

At least my paranoia had faded. I had been taking medication since the hospitalization at North Carolina. I was pretty much fine, despite everything, from the end of November 1990 until January 1996. Five years and two months. I had continued to see the psychiatrist once a week. Even he didn't see what was coming.

In October of '95, I quit my job at the record store again. I don't even remember the reason. I was just becoming sort of a quitter. My parents never called me a quitter. They were always on my side. Little did I realize but all was leading up to the second wave of hospitalizations. I got another call from USA Up All Night and did an episode for them. In between filming that show and when it aired, I was back in the hospital.

Chapter Seven

On the morning of January 3, 1996, I woke up and, as always, went into my mother's bathroom to take my daily medications. The night before, I had watched Nebraska beat the living hell out of Florida in the championship football game. So, I was happy. I was rooting for Nebraska. The team had a lot of players that had been in trouble. I could relate to that.

As soon as I swallowed my medication, blood rushed to my head and I felt like I was going to die. I scared the hell out of myself and rushed to make myself throw up. What could it have been but the medication? I even wondered if someone had tampered with my medication. Why was my reaction so different from one morning to the next? I was sure my life was in danger. Somebody must have been tampering with my medicine. I couldn't stop screaming, "I've got to go to the doctor, I've got to go to the doctor." I went outside, stood on my driveway and began yelling that I was going to die.

The doctor was fifteen minutes from my home. My mother rushed me there in the car. The doctor couldn't tell what was wrong and said I was okay, that she couldn't tell why I would have had such a reaction. The psychiatrist knew about my drinking, but didn't think the alcohol had caused the reaction to the medication. I'd never mentioned using marijuana or crack cocaine. My family felt I just had a bad reaction to the medication and that I was having an anxiety attack. But, as far as I was concerned, I didn't understand how it could have such a drastic effect. To this day, I believe someone tampered with my medication and that is why the second wave of hospitalizations began.

My mother and I drove to a shopping center after seeing the doctor, and I was still feeling sick and nauseous. I felt lightheaded and had to open the car door, because I needed fresh air badly. I felt like I had to throw up again, but I didn't. My God, what just happened? Paranoia kicked in again. Was someone out to get me, messing with my medication? I was really scared. Someone must have wanted to harm me, maybe even kill me. I had no idea who could have been tampering with my medication. It was always kept in my mother's bathroom, and no one in my family would do such a thing. But maybe the pharmacist made a mistake? I wasn't imagining everything and believed I needed to be protected from society. Suddenly, I forgot how bad it was the first time around, and the only safe place for me seemed to be the hospital.

That afternoon, I went to my psychiatrist and pleaded with him to put me in the hospital for protection. I was in a state of panic, because I believed my life was in danger. I never thought I'd ever end up in the hospital again. It was impulsive of me to believe that was my only choice. I shouldn't have insisted, but in my panic I made a mistake again and now was entering the second wave of hospitalizations.

When I arrived at the hospital, I was alone at first, but then a lot of patients suddenly came onto the unit. What the hell was going on? I never felt good about being there and had to battle to make phone calls on the pay phone. Finally, I got through to my psychiatrist, who drove through a nasty snowstorm to see me. I remember watching the snow melt on his boots, as he fought to get me out. By the next evening, I was released.

That night, when I got home, I tried to overdose on a bunch of pills. I kept thinking to myself, "I can't take this anymore." I saw no end to being in the system, so I should just end it all. I had the feeling that people wanted me dead. Before the reaction to the pills, I had never wanted to kill myself, only end the situation. This time I wanted my life to end. The idea of being back in the hospital was too much to handle.

My parents kept trying to stop me. I kept trying to take more and more pills. It was mayhem. Finally, I said, "Screw it!" and decided to just go to sleep and try to start over again in the morning. I would go with the process. Somehow I knew that eventually I would get myself straightened out, and I did, but it took a lot.

The next morning, I didn't feel like moving. I was psychologically messed up from the physical reaction to the drugs. My mother insisted I see my psychiatrist, even though I was feeling too lethargic and asked to wait to see him the next day. Despite my protests, my parents drove me to see him anyway.

In my lethargy, I said perhaps I should go back to the hospital, because I didn't feel well mentally or physically and didn't think I could function on the outside. So, I was admitted to another hospital. After processing the paperwork, I was taken to the unit. People were heavily medicated and walking around like zombies, and I couldn't think straight. I felt like I was in a concentration camp. How was I going to get out of this one? I finally did, thank God. It's why I'm writing this book. But much more would have to happen before I found the true freedom I'd always been seeking.

I knew I had to be in the hospital, but I didn't want to be a zombie like the others, so I didn't always take my medication. But then I couldn't sleep. So, I'd go to the nurses' station and get a sleeping pill. My mother kept a little notebook at the time: "November 29, 1997. All symptoms back: people are controlling his life; people are reading his mind; TV pertains to him; the world is on his shoulders; friends want bad things to happen to him. Paranoid schizophrenic. Impulse control. Delusions of reference. Pervasive developmental disorder." I would endure seventeen different hospitalizations in seven different hospitals, five for a day or less. I'd live at home, live at a motel, live in hospitals. It felt like a never-ending revolving door.

Over the next two months, I was in and out of the same hospital three times. When I was out, I was required to attend a six week outpatient program, with classes and job training, which I never completed, though I attempted to finish it three or four times. The program wasn't that bad, but it wasn't like being on the outside because of being with other patients, some of whom were okay and some not.

My parents couldn't handle me living at home, because they felt I was being destructive towards them or towards myself. I put them through tough times, which I feel a little guilty about. Once, I hit my mother in the car for making me go to the hospital again. She had on a big heavy fur coat and still had a huge bruise on her arm. Against the hospital's advise, she'd taken me out, then forced me to go to the doctor. I was furious. I felt so drugged out and very, very messed up. I just wanted to sleep and said I would go the next day, but she insisted. That time, they put me right back in the hospital, unfortunately.

So my parents paid for me to stay by myself at a nearby motel. One of the reasons I kept going in and out of the hospital was because

I had nowhere to go. The motel was better than the hospital, except for when the weather was cold. The motel room was freezing in the winter, because they couldn't get any heat in there. I couldn't stay out of the hospital living in that horrible motel. It was too uncomfortable. I had to check myself into the hospital just so I could be warm. I even looked for a job to be able to afford a different place to stay that was better than the motel. A nearby gas station seemed to want to hire me and I was all psyched up, but the next morning they said they weren't giving me the job. I was really disappointed and didn't know what to do.

I kept calling my parents, asking them if I could come home, but they said no I couldn't. "We'll pay for the motel, but you're not coming home." One night I came home and literally got on my hands and knees begging them to let me come home, but they wouldn't let me. They didn't want me getting physically violent with my brother, who was still living at home. They were also worried that I would get violent with them. They said you either stay in the motel or go back to the hospital. It was really hard for them to tell me that. I was paranoid, but that wasn't the reason I was hospitalized. I was getting treatment on the outside. They just figured I was safer being hospitalized. Of course, they weren't the ones being hospitalized.

Finally, one of the social workers showed me a brochure for a residence home, and I thought that it didn't look so bad. But, when I got there I found out I didn't have a car, and I didn't have a phone. I had to use the pay phone in the lobby and call collect. I was constantly trying to scrounge up change to make calls. The place was horrible, mostly an old-age home. Every day I was picked up to go to the outpatient program and then returned in the evening. After three days, I just said, "Screw it," I will go back into the hospital, start all over again, and when I get out the next time I will get into a better situation. So I was back in the hospital for three weeks, only to be sent back to the residence home. But, I couldn't adapt to living there.

Each time I went into the hospital, I had the hope that when I got out I would be able to start over, that my problems would finally be gone. I always had that hope. Not only that hope, I just always knew it would happen.

On the soap opera, One Life to Live, there was a character, Todd Manning played by Roger Howarth, who was an inspiration to me. Todd was about my age and wore his hair like me. He was also a college athlete, a football player. I didn't look up to him for getting into trouble, but because he was a lot like me and I could relate to him. At one point, he sustained an injury by getting hit with a weapon and had a big scar on his face. The scar on his face was like the scar on my wrist. While in jail, he was admitted to the prison hospital after getting injured. I could relate, because the prison hospital was similar to a psychiatric hospital. He was smart. He escaped from jail and saved the life of the girl, who was the defendant against him when he got locked up in the first place. As a result of rescuing her life, he was given a hearing and then a pardon. Then, he inherited a lot of money and started wheeling and dealing. He was going through tough times and trying to get things straightened out, just like I was. I needed to watch him in order to believe I could turn my life around like he did.

During the in between times before the second wave, I didn't have any wild behavior like what was to happen during the second wave. But, during the second wave, when I was twenty-six and twenty-seven, impulsive trips got me into a lot of trouble. I was a loose cannon, taking off to San Juan, St. Thomas, Florida and Buffalo.

My parents never knew what to expect from day to day, never knew what to expect whenever the phone rang. Everywhere I went, I would call my mother. She'd stay home out of fear that she would miss my call and be unable to avoid a tragedy. Though I don't remember, she said there were times when I was completely irrational. Other times I would call in the midst of a panic attack or when I was feeling paranoid.

My first trip was to San Juan, Puerto Rico. My destination was actually St. Thomas, but I didn't get that far. Each time I left, my motive was to look for a new place and a fresh start. Finding a job and a place to stay would be easy I thought, and I would be able to begin a new life. My parents couldn't stop me from going, because I had my own money from work. As I waited in the San Juan airport for the connecting flight to St. Thomas, I panicked and began to break down. I followed the ticket agent all around, telling her my whole life story. She had to have been thinking, "This guy's crazy." I felt like people were yelling at me. Paranoid thoughts. So, I got in a cab and told the driver to take me to the nearest hotel. He brought me to a nice hotel. Luckily I had money. I registered and got to my room as quickly as I could, where I was able to calm down a bit. After ordering room service, I called my father and pleaded with him to come down and get me. The next morning, my father and uncle both arrived and brought me back home, with the stipulation that when I got back home, I would check myself into the hospital.

On the flight going back home, I made a plan to make it all the way to St. Thomas in the near future. I wasn't feeling too messed up. I didn't even feel I needed to go to the hospital, though they said I did. It was only a few weeks before I was again out of the hospital and on my way to St. Thomas. This time I made it all the way. After checking into the hotel, I went to their bar and had a couple of beers. I met a guy there, and we went back to the room and smoked pot.

The next morning, I woke up with a severe headache, and I told myself I couldn't be doing that any more. It wasn't healthy. I was twenty-seven, so enough already. And that was the last time I ever smoked weed.

That same morning, I stood watching some kids playing basketball. Their coach was a black man with dread locks. Finally, I asked them if I could play, and they started laughing at me. It was because I looked drugged out, like I had a bad hangover, which I did. For the next few days, I looked for a job and went shopping. But, then I was feeling the pressure of being away from home. So, I flew back. When I landed at LaGuardia Airport, I just hopped in a cab and left my luggage at the airport. Somehow, my parents got my luggage for me the next day, and I was back in the hospital.

When I got out of that hospitalization, I contacted a friend in Florida, who thought he could get me a job at a sports club. On the way down, I would drive for a few hours, then find a Holiday Inn and sleep for a few hours. My parents kept wiring me money. When I arrived, it turned out that my friend did offer me a job. But, I had no place free to stay and had to stay in a motel. Turned out that later my mother sent extra money to the woman who owned the motel, as a thank you for being such a help to me. Mom sent a lot of people a lot of money for taking special care of me, when they didn't have to.

Finally, I realized I probably couldn't hold a job anyway, so I turned around and headed back home. The trip back from Florida seemed endless. There were stretches of road with only trees and fields where I felt, if I stalled out, I'd never find help and possibly could have never been found and died. As on the way down, I made frequent stops at Holiday Inns just to sleep for a few hours. My medication could have been making me tired. This time, when I came home, my parents put me in a room at the local motel, instead of in the hospital.

In 1994, in between the first and second waves of hospitalizations, I'd gone to Toronto with my brother and a friend. I'd had a good time there and so decided, "Why not try Toronto?" So, in the dead of winter, I decided to see if I could start a new life in Toronto. I took a train, but got off in Buffalo, suddenly certain that if I went over the border I could have a tough time getting back into the country. When I got off in Buffalo, I found a room, ordered a pizza and set off to find a job in a couple of retail stores. No one would hire me. The temperature was sub zero, and I didn't have a hat or gloves or scarf. I was amazed my ears didn't freeze off. I was calling my mother all the time. She was scared that I would have frostbite, as I waited in the train station to head back home. Whenever I left for somewhere, I was always sure everything would work out. After returning, I nearly always ended up back in the hospital.

Cars figured in lots of unfortunate incidents. Once, I left a car in the middle of the West Side Highway in Manhattan, because I ran out of gas and because I was drunk. I didn't know how to pump gas myself. Someone, who worked at a body shop off the highway, called my Mom and said I was there. As always, she hopped in the car. On the way, in the early hours of the morning, she ran into a huge traffic jam on the West Side Highway and was certain I had caused it. After getting me home once again, Mom sent the man at the body shop some money for taking care of me.

One time, I headed for Florida again and, after asking for directions at a toll booth, ended up in Massachusetts instead. The car got wrecked and had to be left there. Each time I left home, I was so sure I would be making a new start and everything was going to turn out all right. That's all I wanted.

But, finally I saw no ending to all I was dealing with. I never wanted to kill myself. I just wanted all my problems to end. But, sadly, they were far from over.

CHAPTER EIGHT

Gunhill Road in the Bronx seemed like an appropriate place. When I spotted three guys in their late teens, who looked like they could get their hands on what I was looking for, I pulled over to the side of the road, rolled down my window and said, "I'll give you my car, if you get me a gun."

They climbed into my brand new Nissan Sentra. I didn't have any money at the time, so the car was all I had to offer. They got into the car, and we drove around in search of a gun. At one point, I had to go to the bathroom, so we pulled over to a service station, and while I was in there they took off with the car. I found a nearby police station, which was close to Yankee Stadium, and told the cops what happened. Seeing the state I was in, they handcuffed me and took me to a nearby hospital, where I stayed for a couple of hours, until they transferred me to a hospital closer to where I lived. A few days later, the police found my car and it was trashed. The whole car had to be repaired.

The mental and physical suffering was intensifying. My mental suffering would never end it seemed. Physically, I had no energy to stay in shape, something that had been so important to me. I felt I was wasting away. I was living in hell, constantly surrounded by people both old and young who weren't well themselves, either physically or mentally. I was surrounded by illness 24/7. No one would have wanted to be in such a situation. And, I had lost my freedom, which had always been priceless to me. Now I never knew when I would be getting out of a hospitalization when I went into one or where I would be going when I did get out. I was caught in a revolving door.

On April 3, 1997, I called a friend, Paul, and told him I needed a favor. I'd been out of the hospital for five and a half months- free but for various reasons I was seeing one psychiatrist after another, was on medication and still involved with drinking and drugs. I wasn't working a good job. My only pleasurable activities were lifting weights and playing basketball. Basically, I saw no end to my situation, to the personal torment and to being in the system. I thought I was okay. It was just that the system didn't agree with my assessment. But, I really wasn't okay.

Paul met me outside his house. He walked up to my car and got in. "Get me a gun, I want to kill myself," I told him. "Hold on a second," Paul said, then got out of the car and went back inside his house.

Paul hung out with friends of mine from high school, which is how I got to know him. We'd go out and party. He was heavily into drugs and a hard-core drinker, much worse than I was. I smoked crack cocaine with him, which I began to prefer over marijuana, because crack cocaine was an upper where weed was a downer. In one of my previous hospitalizations, Paul had arrived at the hospital unit with a bag from McDonald's, and in the paper cup was beer. I didn't drink it.

Paul had hired me to work for him a few times a week. He repaired furniture, and I did odd jobs for him, whatever he needed me to do. He made house calls to repair furniture and I came with him sometimes. I had no idea what I was doing, but he instructed me. He paid me very well, seventy dollars a day, better than the six or seven an hour I was used to being paid. But, he was erratic. Sometimes, I'd go to his house to work, and he'd be sleeping it off. After work, he'd go to the liquor store and buy a fifth of Jack Daniels.

As I waited for Paul to come back out of his house with a gun for me, I suddenly heard sirens and a couple of police cars pulled up beside me. After seeing me, they called the ambulance. The ambulance took me to the admitting room of a hospital, where I almost got into a fight. My parents met me there. I wasn't mad at Paul for betraying me. What was he supposed to do, really?

So, I was admitted again, after being free for five and a half months. As always, my parents visited every day. Two weeks after Paul had called the cops and I was hospitalized again, my mother got a call from his mother: "He's gone. Paul's gone." Mom rushed over to their house, and a workman confirmed that someone had just died. Paul was twenty-seven and died of walking pneumonia. My parents came over to the hospital to tell me, and I started crying. Maybe I had something to do with it? But, I'd been in the hospital for twelve days, so how could I be responsible? But I felt so bad. It was such a tragedy.

This was an extremely difficult hospitalization. I was violent-trashed my room a couple of times and got into a few fights, some in self defense. I got into scuffles with the mental health workers. One worker, who had a patch over one eye, gave me a hard time, and I told him I was going to knock out his other eye. I was strapped to a table after that. The arguing always got me switched to a different unit. One time I went into the bathroom, trying to get the attention of the mental health workers, and cut both sides of my face with a plastic knife. They had said they were going to be right with me, but I couldn't wait. Luckily the wounds healed just like they said they would.

With all my fighting, I was always holding my own and I was proud of that. I lost very few fights. Even in a boxing class I had taken a few years before everything went badly, I held my own with some really tough people. I'd grown up fighting. When I had to, I usually got the better of people, even in the hospitals. I still think having that broken leg my freshman year was what turned me into a fighter. I became an angry, unhappy person for the rest of high school. Of course, my brothers and I would fight growing up. I was the youngest and always had to defend myself. I think that carried over and made me sort of a hard nosed, tough kind of kid. My brothers were a lot bigger and older than I was, but I always held my own.

One kid in particular kept on giving me a hard time and getting me into trouble. He would not leave me alone, and I was unable to back down. I was twenty-seven, and he was in his late teens and a skin head. It was as if someone had paid him off to get me into trouble, and he got me into a lot of trouble. He was relentless. He would instigate fights, get in my face and give me a hard time. He had to be getting paid off, otherwise why would he be getting into my face? I didn't want to do anything to him physically, because the consequences would be severe. But I couldn't help myself, I felt as if I had to defend myself. So I was sent to another psychiatric hospital for more intensive treatment.

I was strapped down on a stretcher when they transported me to the new place by ambulance. I was well aware of what it meant to be sent there. Some patients stayed ten, twenty years, even for life. It was much harder to get out once admitted. The hospital had a notorious history. The old buildings were decrepit and not even used any more. But I was never placed in a unit where people were catatonic or knocking their heads against the walls. The units where I was kept were pretty bad, but not like in the movie One Flew Over the Cuckoo's Nest. If I were in a place like that, I'd probably never have gotten out.

The first unit I was placed in was coed. On a mixed unit, it is important to be careful with the other patients, so that there aren't any false accusations about improper behavior. However, I did continue to have physical disputes with other male patients and staff members.

I was constantly on the phone to my parents to get me out of there. The phone calls also gave me a sense of contact with the outside world. One night, when I was talking with my parents, a doctor kept interrupting the call and telling me to get off the phone because it was after hours. He was behind a high desk at the nurses' station and started yelling at me. So, I jumped over the desk, and when he put his hand up to his face to defend himself, I injured his finger and was thrown onto the secure unit.

Being on the secure unit meant I could not get out of the hospital under any circumstances, period. No patient could be discharged from the hospital from that unit ever. At that realization, I panicked like I'd never panicked before. I was scared to death imagining what it would be like to never get out of there. I was sure I was going to be there for years, if not for life. What was I going to do? But, as it turned out, they only kept me in that unit for one day. One really crazy patient walked up to me and grabbed me by the neck and kept trying to choke me, and I had to defend myself. This was one of the lowest points of my life.

But the staff on the secure unit quickly realized that I was more advanced than all the other patients. I was a college graduate in a place like that. So after a day, I was transferred to an all male unit, which ended up being of great benefit to me and the turning point of my life. The social workers were easier to deal with and over the next months worked hard to get me well and out of there.

My parents visited every day as always and brought me good food, and I connected with one guy, a staff member, with whom I passed the time watching baseball and football on television. But that was the extent of any real companionship. We had three meals a day and a snack at night. Once a day, a staff member would bring us off the unit to purchase food and sodas from the vending machine. During the week I attended groups. When the weather was nice, we went outside in an enclosed fenced in area, and I mostly watched the cars drive by. Once in a while, I would smoke a cigarette. But, I struggled every day. This was a more intensive hospital, and the older I got the less chance I felt I had of ever leaving the place. Time was running out for me.

Each day in the hospital, when I saw my psychiatrist, I'd ask the same question, "When am I getting out of here?" I began working even harder with my two social workers to get me to a place to get out, even if I had to go on the grounds. At least then I could work from the day program and be halfway free. As from the beginning of my ordeals in North Carolina, I had to have my freedom. I had to get out of there. I'd say to myself, "Don't tell them that you're not feeling well. Get out, and once you get out, seek treatment. First, get out."

At night, I'd go up to some of the mental health workers and talk with them. I'd tell them my plans for when I was getting out and ask them when they thought that might be. They didn't know, and that was tough.

I wasn't planning to escape. The idea just came upon me. Suddenly, I walked right by one of the workers standing by the security doors.

When he stopped me, I told him I was one of the workers. So, I walked right past him and out of the hospital. I had ten dollars in change and went first to find a pay phone to call a friend and see if I could hide out there. He wasn't home, so I got a cab and went to the motel where I used to stay and got a room. Then I went to a nearby Dunkin' Donuts and got a really delicious drink. My father and uncle came to be with me at the motel. Just when I was about to go to sleep, there was a knocking on the door, and it was the cops. I had to go back.

At some point in the day I had called my mother. The hospital had called her to tell her of my escape, and she told them not to worry, that I would call her soon because I always did. Otherwise, the police would have been searching for me and the story of my escape would have been all over the news.

Finally, on January 22, 1998, I was discharged to an outpatient facility on the hospital grounds, after being in the hospital since June. At least I was somewhat free. I could go home every weekend. I could come and go as I pleased. There was a place to buy food, candy and stuff and I had money, so I was able to buy those things. Some of the people, who were in the day program, were nice and pretty together. I had a little job, where I made a little money. I was making progress. But I wasn't happy there.

On February 9, I took a bus to Grand Central Station and ended up going to my brother's apartment in the city. It was a mess. My mother and Dad rushed into the city in a panic. My mother got lost on the way, ending up in a gas station where no one spoke English. She was wedged between two cars, but jumped out of hers and somehow got directions. After picking me up at my brother's apartment, my parents took me directly to one of my previous hospitals, where I was put in the holding area until the next morning, when they told me I was accepted back to the hospital grounds from where I had escaped. Something in me finally clicked and this would turn out to be my last hospitalization.

CHAPTER NINE

The next day, February 10, while I was in the holding area, they told me I could go back into the day program, if that's what I wanted.

The understanding had been growing that I only had one more chance to turn my life around, or I would be in the system forever. If my behavior warranted my return to the hospital, I would be facing years of confinement. As I sat in the holding area, I could clearly see this was my moment of choice. Which way would I let my life go? Would I be free or live in captivity? All that was required of me to be free was that I cooperate with authorities and stop drinking and doing drugs, otherwise I would forever be struggling mentally. I would be in the system for many years and wouldn't have a chance for a happy life. After I made the decision to quit doing harm to myself mentally and physically, I knew I had to do everything I could to get myself on track. With that understanding, I realized I didn't need to hang out with my old friends, who just wanted to keep the partying going. I never did do drugs or alcohol to cover up pain, and I never was addicted. Addicted means you can't stop, and I was always able to do what I had to in life. I just liked to party too much.

So, I decided I was going to take my life seriously. I finally understood what I needed for myself, a conclusion I came to on my own. Facing the inevitable, I chose to start all over again, to start my life anew. I had one more chance and I had to capitalize on it. I went cold turkey, turned my life completely around and did everything I needed to do to get better. I consider February 10, 1998 my new birth date. Though I was twenty-eight-years-old, I was reborn in that holding area, and now as I write I consider myself to be nine years old, as it's been nine years since my last hospitalization and the last time I ever drank or used drugs.

The system straightened me out eventually, but I wonder if I really needed to go through all the hospitalizations. To me, it was like going to jail, getting out and then going back. Jail is more dangerous, but you know the time period for when you're getting out. The second wave was a wake up call about where I could be heading for the rest of my life. Did I really want to keep coming back to hospital after hospital? In a way it was how someone would think of prison, if someone were in and out of the system for lengthier periods of time. So, if I ended up back in the hospital after being there six months, I could do more time, even ten years later, like for a repeat offense. There are people I was there with that might still be there after nine years.

When I looked at my hospitalizations, I put myself on the level of Mike Tyson, Darryl Strawberry, Dwight Gooden, Jean Claude Van Damme, Don Imus, Dave Mustaine (the lead singer of Megadeth), James Frey- people who are very, very advanced and they ended up in these places, but are now well enough to stay out. All were able to straighten themselves out. A lot of people I looked up to were around in the eighties. For a while, during my troubles, I didn't think of them. But then when I started getting myself together I could reintegrate them. All but one of Mötley Crüe has been in prison. There were a lot of them. When Dave Mustaine was in Metallica, the other members kicked him out of the band and gave him a bus ticket from New York to San Francisco. He finally started his own smaller band- kind of like my going from North Carolina to a small school in New York.

It seemed like I was a card carrying member of what I called the "generation without freedom." A lot of important people ended up behind the eight ball as far as hospitalizations or jail. That's how I feel about the nineties- a backwards kind of a generation. The eighties were a big time for drugs. In the nineties it became a situation that we didn't know how to handle. Roddy Piper was the only person I could look up to. In the eighties, I looked up to Dwight Gooden. Then he ended up in rehab in '87, right after they'd won the World Series. Darryl Strawberry- spring semester at North Carolina, I saw him in spring training and he'd just gotten out of rehab. He was very narrow minded. Mike Tyson got into trouble because of his stature. They all ended up behind bars or in hospitals. I also knew a lot of people that ended up messed up like that. It happened to them, then it happened to me. When these people reached their mid thirties, it started to straighten out a little bit.

Because I kept myself out of the hospital and out of legal troubles for nine months, I was upgraded in October to being allowed to live off grounds. Before then, I'd lived on the grounds of the hospital, going to a daily program, working in the kitchen and going home on weekends. I often ate dinner in the cafeteria or at the pizza place just off the grounds. Being on the grounds was so much better than being an inpatient. I made a few friends, staff workers as well as patients. One staff member, who worked on my inpatient unit, went with me to a Yankee game and a college basketball game.

I began working with a new social worker, who was very nice and got me into a halfway house in a nearby town. I was advised not to live at home at first. Life at the halfway house wasn't very structured, so I learned to handle my freedom. I could watch my progress as my freedom increased and there was less monitoring. I was feeling more and more in control of myself and more and more straightened out. The new medication I was on was working.

Every day, I was picked up by a van at the halfway house and driven to an outpatient program then driven back in the afternoon. My dad and uncle would pick me up at the halfway house and take me home, and I'd lift weights, watch sports and music videos, listen to music and study. Sometimes my mom would take me to the mall. Wednesday nights I had to be at the halfway house, because it was my job to cook dinner that night of the week. Wednesdays were the worst days for me, because all my time was spent involved with the program. Friday afternoons were the best, because I was able to be at home on the weekends.

I began to make plans and set goals for myself and realized I wanted to return to school for a graduate degree. Others believed I wasn't ready, but I was determined and I did it, taking one class a semester. I had been taking a class at a local college in the summer of '96 toward a graduate degree in Criminal Justice, the same degree as my undergraduate major. In fact, I had come home from San Juan and took a final, so I had three credits and needed thirty to graduate. Taking one class a semester, including the summer sessions, which was all I could handle, I got my masters in three years. I wasn't in a rush, because my life kept getting better and better, both mentally and physically. Though the odds were against me, given my psychiatric history, I wanted to become a New York City police officer.

My life made another shift for the better. I had continued working hard with my social worker, and in late March 2000 I got really lucky and was allowed to move to a fairly nice, supervised apartment, in a good area only minutes from the program. Living on my own, finally, meant I had even more freedom and responsibility for my life. I shared the apartment with one other guy. My schedule was pretty much the same as it was when I was living in the halfway house, but I began to feel more normal. The worst of my misery was behind me. The years I'd spent in the system had been brutally hard at times. But the constant struggle of my inpatient days was truly over. I was really making progress. My life was pretty good. Even the problems we had with the new apartment were nothing compared to what I'd been through. Clogged sinks and bad plumbing were annoying enough, though, that my parents finally let me move back home for good. I was absolutely ecstatic to be living at home. Now all my suffering was truly over.

After earning my masters degree at the end of 2001, I tried to get a job in the criminal justice field. While I was preparing to take the exam for the NYPD, I got a job at a local gym, working part time while I continued the outpatient program. Working there was better than most of the jobs I'd had, because I was in my element by being in a physical fitness environment. I liked my supervisors and the people I worked with. I never worked out there, though. Working out elsewhere had become my daily routine, which was important to maintain. I was progressing and began working more hours, from nine to three Monday through Friday. All was working out well. But, after working there for thirteen months, my hours were changed because of budget cuts, and I worked only Saturdays and Sundays. Eventually, I was let go.

Again, I prepared to take the exam for the NYPD and landed a job at a local clothing store in the meantime. That job lasted five weeks. I was dismissed because I simply couldn't get the basics down, like finding clothes in their confusing stock room, and I had problems restocking the store. My supervisor there told me I was a nice guy, just unable to adjust to the job. I was actually relieved, because I didn't like the fact that my hours were different every week. Right after that, I got a job at a local sporting goods store, which I have kept until this day.

The loss of the two jobs were setbacks, and I experienced two more major ones. Despite obtaining a security guard's license, I was unable to find a security job. And, I went through the whole process, passing the tests, but was turned down by the NYPD. According to the rejection letter, I didn't meet their requirements, which had to mean that my psychological background was not acceptable. Despite the setbacks, I never got discouraged. Being turned down by the NYPD was probably the best thing, because I wasn't really sure if I could handle the stress of being a police officer.

After being turned down by the NYPD, I seriously considered joining the French Foreign Legion, something I had been fascinated by since I was young. I liked the fact that they were known to stand by their soldiers and give them a second and third chance. They also accepted people who had had problems in their lives and turned to the Legion for a brand new start. The Legion was also known for the camaraderie of its soldiers, and that appealed to me. I did a lot of research and discovered I qualified, but the more I thought about it, the more I realized the five-year commitment might be difficult to keep, and I wasn't sure if I wanted to go to France and leave everything behind.

Meanwhile, I rejoined the gym in 2001 and began to lift weights seriously again. Since joining, I have kept up my practice, lifting two hours a session anywhere from four to six days a week. I have two workouts. Two to three days a week, I bench press for my chest, pull downs for my back, shoulder presses, crunches for my stomach and the stationary bicycle for my cardiovascular system. The other two to three days a week, I do curling for my biceps, pushdowns for my triceps, thigh presses, calf raises and again stomach and cardio exercises.

I took up boxing classes again from October to December of 2002. I also took Shihouken Karate from January to November of 2005, and went from white to blue belt. One of the main reasons I decided to take karate was the influence of martial arts expert, Jean Claude Van Damme, one of my favorite actors. I always admired the characters he played in his movies, usually rough cut, physically tough people, who possessed "street knowledge." I liked how he always came out on top of his enemies and any opposition. Jean Claude Van Damme gave me the motivation to take karate consistently for ten months. But the karate was a struggle at times. The three instructors were good, but I had a tough time picking it up and finally decided to quit, because my level of talent wasn't as good as it needed to be.

In 2000, I decided I wanted to play baseball again. Though I hadn't played in years, I still believed I had it in me to play well. I have played in an amateur league each season since, though some years I couldn't commit to the entire season. My best season so far was 2004, when I batted over .300, going 10 for 31. As an outfielder, I do consistently well. The team has always had a losing record, but there have been some wins and a few big ones.

For five days in January 2004, I fulfilled one of my dreams by participating in the New York Mets fantasy camp, which was held in Port St. Lucie, Florida. We started with drills and played a total of eight games with eight different teams. The teams were managed by former major leaguers, and the camp ended with a game against the former major leaguers. In June, we played a reunion game at Shea Stadium, which was great. I went two for three.

After being turned down by the NYPD, I decided to try acting again. First I took a class to get back into it, then got my headshots made and then began to weekly mail them to all the prime time shows, soap operas and various other casting directors. The most notable work I got was the movie "Tenderness" and the television comedy 30 Rock, which made me eligible for a Screen Actors Guild membership. I am already in AFTRA.

In August of 2002, I was able to leave the psychiatric program for good. Since then, I just see a psychologist and a psychiatrist once every two weeks. It's difficult to know, but somehow I feel, that if I had accepted psychiatric counseling the summer of 1990, when everything began unraveling, and put myself on some medication for a little while, maybe I would have been okay. When I got to the point of telling the doctors I wanted to kill myself, it was too late. Here I'd had the opportunity before that to seek treatment. That would have been the right thing to do. But, how would I know? I had no experience with mental illness. Not until after the second wave of hospitalizations did I again realize what okay was.

CHAPTER TEN

It's been nine years now, since I was in that holding area and faced with a choice that most people wouldn't have thought that I even had. Given how out of control I was, no one thought I was capable of pulling myself together, much less getting out of the system altogether. But, I am better now than ever, and I will never be institutionalized again. Never, never again. I've learned my lesson, believe me. My parents think it is a miracle. Others say it is the medicine. But I believe my healing came about because I called on my higher will, and found the strength to give up my old ways and become a brand new person who has contributed and continues to contribute to society.

I had ten years of experimentation, which isn't bad compared to a lot of people. Lots of people in recovery can say they were doing drugs or drinking for twenty-five years, easily. I've learned that marijuana is a downer. It messes your mind up, makes you feel slow and begins to make you feel like a loser. Towards the last few times I did it, I just felt like a loser. Crack cocaine makes you feel so high and energetic. You feel really good. But, I don't support drug use at all now. It's been ten years, since I've taken any drugs. I don't drink beer or smoke. I did take up cigarettes for a little while when I was an outpatient. What the hell, everyone was smoking. Since I turned twenty-seven, nothing. The only AA meeting I went to was acting in one for two episodes on the soap opera Guiding Light. No drug meetings. No outside help. I did it on my own. I just said, "This is enough. I'm not doing this any more." Maybe someone reading this book will be helped. They will see I've been through the scene and I have an insight. Maybe they will consider quitting and realize "I don't have to do this either." It could help somebody. It really could.

What I went through was a horrible experience, but I made a lot of changes. I want people to realize how incredibly difficult it is to go through mental illness and hospitalizations, so that they can be understanding of someone in their lives who may be going through a similar experience. I paid my dues and paid my debt to society for some of the things I did. But it was very difficult. It wasn't a joke. The debt, I'm sure, was for some of my violent behavior. Many people did similar things and got away free with no repercussions. I would rather I didn't have to go through what I did, but I am reborn because of my experiences. At this point in my life, I have to believe that everything turned out for the best, though I wouldn't have known it at the time I was going through everything. I can write this book now. Things do turn out for the best. I can help other people that are in the same situation I was in.

My father's younger brother has been in an outpatient program his whole life for being mentally ill. He's in his seventies now. That fact was kept hidden from my mother when she was talking about marriage with my dad and my dad's family. I visited my uncle a few times. He's a nice guy. He's not retarded or anything, but he needs to be supervised. If he were in regular society, he wouldn't be able to work. He wouldn't be able to take care of himself that way.

I don't believe my problems were genetic. I was just a time bomb ready to explode. My anger got me into trouble, but it could have gotten me into even worse trouble. I could have gotten into more trouble with the law. In hindsight, though I used to think the opposite, I'm lucky that I've never been in jail or prison. I've been locked up in mental hospitals, but never locked up in jail. That would be a stigma.

My story is about a guy who has gone through a lot. But, he's conquered all his struggles and now can do whatever he wants. He lives in a nice home, works and is a good athlete. Look at what he's been through and look at what he's able to do now. My story will hopefully inspire others. If I had never been hospitalized, if I'd graduated from North Carolina with no real problems, I think I would have been okay. But, the first hospitalization, the in-between period until the next wave of hospitalizations, and then the next wave, of course I wish it all had never happened. Not only was it a costly emotional experience for me and all who loved me, I also lost a good inheritance. The thirty thousand dollars I was due to inherit on my next birthday, the one after my admittance to the first mental hospital in North Carolina, was all used to pay for my care. But, it was used to make me well, which was the most important thing. Now I can make something good out of my troubles.

If I'd stayed in New York for school, instead of going to North Carolina, the drugs and drinking might have continued, which it did for years. I don't know what might have happened. Now, if I were in high school, I would join the French Foreign Legion, instead of going to college. That would have given me more of a worldly experience. But, it took twenty years out of high school to gain that hindsight.

Everything's been really good for the last nine years. I was reborn when I left the last hospitalization. I started my life over, a brand new person. I told myself I was going to get serious and quit the drinking, quit the drugs. Now I don't condone pot smoking at all, nor the use of any drugs. Instead of partying, I concentrated on school, concentrated on work, concentrated on athletics, and got back into acting. I'd wanted to be part of the NYPD, but unfortunately my past hospitalizations prevented me. I don't blame them. I went through the process, but when they gave me the psychiatric test I was turned down. I was happy I went through the process, though. It showed that I had perseverance.

The thing I am most happy about is that my physical health is perfect. I'm an athlete. Look at someone like Dwight Gooden, Darryl Strawberry or Mike Tyson. I can relate to them. They're still physically able to do anything they want, even after all their problems. Dwight Gooden, the pitcher, just got out of prison. He's forty-one years old. My story is for athletes, people who have been hospitalized, college students. Athletes would say, boy this guy has gotten to a level where it's just about as good as it gets. I lift weights, play amateur ball, I'm going to start playing basketball again. As far as I am concerned, I feel that from the age twenty-eight on, I built a new life. I started over again and just don't act like I used to, though many of my interests like sports and music are the same. I have no idea what my old drinking buddies are doing now. I haven't seen most of them for fifteen or sixteen years. For the last nine years, I haven't seen anybody.

I haven't been reborn in the religious sense, because I'm not at all religious. I never had a desire to "turn myself over to God," or join the Moonies or Jehovah's Witnesses. Not even close. I'm still listening to the satanic heavy metal music, the angry hip hop. I'm still into the same music: death metal, thrash metal, hip hop, free style- all that kind of stuff. If someone asks if I believe in God, I say, "Yes," though the music I listen to promotes satanism. I love the music. I listen to it, but I'm not satanic. Some people take the satanic stuff so seriously they join satanic cults or antichrist cults. They take it to the extreme.

But, most of the people that listen to the music just like it for the music. I listen to the music but don't practice what they preach. Now, I'm a straightedge kind of guy. In fact, Straight Edge music means music without drinking, smoking or doing drugs, something I can now relate to.

A lot of good people have helped me and my family over the years, some you wouldn't expect like the people at the record store. When I worked there, I had some severe panic attacks. Lots could happen in the middle of a panic attack, but they always let me leave if I needed to and never fired me.

This year, as I write my book, is my nine year anniversary of getting out of the hospital. There's really no spectacular ending to my story. I'm just doing what I have to and what I enjoy. I'm still living happily at home with my parents. I work part-time, lift weights full-time, and do my mailings every week to various New York casting directors. I still have a rooting interest in sports. But now my favorite major college basketball team is the Duke Blue Devils.

My goals and standards are very high for the future. I'm in a very fortunate position, because I am extremely healthy physically, with all of the exercise I do. I am treated well and very respected at work, at the gym, on my baseball team and at my acting jobs. I had a great experience in graduate school. I live a clean life mentally and physically and I'm confident about what my future holds.

But, the main thing is that I am happy with my life. The one thing that would make me even happier is if the message that this book gives helps other people in a similar situation. I want people to know that it is possible to overcome personal problems or issues, that they can get their life back on track and live happy and successful lives. If things hadn't happened the way they did, maybe I wouldn't have had a book to write that might now help others in my situation.

Who knows where I would have ended up? I am probably in a better place for all of it.

www.ingramcontent.com/pod-product-compliance
Lightning Source LLC
Chambersburg PA
CBHW031242280526
45784CB00004B/1686